Optavia Air Fryer Cookbook 2021-2022

*800-Day Super Easy Air Fryer Recipes
with Fresh Lean and Green Meals for Beginners and Advanced
Help You Keep Healthy and Lose Weight by Harnessing the Power of "Fueling
Hacks Meals"*

Yahol Shabot

Table of Contents

Introduction

The Optavia Air Fryer is definitely for you. Especially Optavia diet, also known as Lean and Green Diet, it is to lose weight diet without feeling hungry. You can easily eat a lot of fish or other lean protein food to lose weight. Lean and green diet method is a very popular diet that is embraced by many people due to its simple and delicious taste and green color.

Optavia Air Fryer is so much more than just a healthy way to enjoy some crispy fried foods without worrying about getting fat. It is an appliance that can cook an incredible variety of dishes, including many that you probably never thought possible.

Eating far too much fried food increases the risk of obesity and overweight. The more fried food you eat, the more likely you will be to develop diabetes. However, if you have meals cooked in Optavia Air Fryer, the problem will not exist. So it's time to turn to air fried food to decrease the fat intake and to lose some weight without reducing your fried food intake. Because air fryer helps to reduce the amount of fat.

Chapter 1: Optavia Diet Basics

What is the Optavia Diet?

The Medifast team are the people that made the Optivia diet, a health and weight loss diet program that requires you to take sometimes 6 meals a day containing their fueling products and small meals called Lean and Green. The team says that if you integrate healthy habits, follow their coach's instructions, and eat according to this diet's nutritional guidelines, including their products, you will see great improvement in your health and wellness.

Fueling products (bars, shakes, etc.) are low-calorie energizing products. Lean and Green meals are meals containing one meat, one vegetable and one healthy fat component. Together they fill your stomach and provide you with ample nutrition with low amounts of calories. You will not lose much muscle mass. There is a high protein option of the diet in which 10% or more portion of the meal is protein.

The diet also cuts carbohydrates so that your body starts using fat as fuel. You will eat about 90g of carbs in this diet. This will make your body use the alternative macronutrient, fat, for energy.

How does Optavia Work?

Most people follow the Optimal Weight 5&1 plan, which results in fast weight loss. You can have five servings of big fueling products in a day. It could be soup, biscuits, puddings, shakes etc. The one signifies a lean green meal. You have to cook meat and eat three servings of non-starchy vegetables like eggplant, tomato, okra, and healthy fats. The fueling products have high levels of protein and probiotics, which keep the gut healthy.

When dieting

you will be in contact with health coaches that will keep you in check and give advice. They will also transition out of the diet when you have reached your goal weight. The company also offers a series of products that will help you maintain weight in the 3&3 plan. You can also choose a more flexible plan 4&2&1 in which you can also eat one snack in between. They will also give you specific products if you suffer from diabetes, are breastfeeding or are aged.

Optavia Diet Programs

The company's products are all labelled with their components. You will get around 70-80 grams of protein, 100 grams of carbohydrates and less than 30% of fat in your fueling foods. You will, on average, consume 40% protein, 40% carbs and 20% healthy fats. The products have all the essential minerals and vitamins according to their recommended amount. The products have high-quality protein and probiotics, which help keep muscles and gut healthy.

There are many variations of the diet, and you will choose from it depending on your preference. Motivational support and encouragement by coaches will be present in all of the plans. You will have an online community that will help you and an app that will remind you of meals and track calories.

5 & 1 Plan

This is the list of the most popular plan that can result in rapid weight loss. You will eat six short meals a day. Five will be the products provided by Medifast and one lean and green meal.

4 & 2 & 1 Plan

This plan has more calories than the previous 5&1 plan. You have to eat four fueling products in a day, 2 lean and green meals and a healthy snack. A snack should be fruits or vegetables.

3 & 3 Plan

This plan needs to be followed after you have reached your ideal weight. To maintain your current weight, the company tells you to consume 3 fueling food and three lean and green meals.

Although there are many types, the diet should not be followed by someone having a chronic illness. Certain people, like breastfeeding mothers, need to take an opinion before starting it.

What to Eat on Optavia Diet?

Food to Eat:

✧ Lean Protein

In an Optivia diet, you need to make at least one lean and green meal that will have lean protein as the main ingredient. Protein is extremely important in maintaining good health and keeping low calories. It is good for skin, lean body mass and encourages satiety. One gram of protein will give you 4 calories and is responsible for the development of immunity, enzymes, hormones and growth. To optimize your experience, you need to choose the best protein source with low calories and fat but high nutrition. Some examples are listed below:

✧ **Fish**

Most fishes have low saturated fatty acids, which are also called bad fats. Fish such as salmon, tuna, mackerel, cod, anchovies are packed with healthy omega 3 fatty acids.

✧ **Chicken and turkey**

Grill, roast, or bake your poultry before eating because it cuts calories. These sources are good but try to opt for a leaner piece of their meat, lighter meat. Their nutritional value can vary, so read the label before use.

✧ **Lean beef**

People think they have cut red meat entirely to eat healthily. If you choose beef with 'round' and 'loin' written on them, you will get less fat and calories for protein. The meat should have low marbling and less visible fat. You can cut the excess fat yourself or by asking your butcher. Always go for the lean and extra lean ground beef options. Try bison if you really like the taste of beef and want to eat more of it.

✧ **Eggs**

Cheap, easy and versatile, eggs are low in calories band filled with protein. There are endless egg dishes you can make without any help.

✧ **Low-fat dairy**

Skimmed milk, low-fat cheese, yogurt and greek yogurt are a must if you are dieting They have less saturated fat and are denser in protein.

✧ **Beans, lentils and peas**

They are a go-to protein source for vegetarians. Try to promote satiety, are filled with fiber and can be added to salads and soups.

✧ **Non-Starchy Vegetables**

Having more vegetables is a part of a healthy diet and can help in protecting you from different diseases. Here are some examples of the best vegetables you can eat:

- Artichoke
- Asparagus
- Bamboo shoots
- Bean sprouts
- Brussel sprouts
- Cabbage
- Carrots

- Cauliflower
- Celery
- Cucumber
- Eggplant
- Leafy green vegetables like kale and spinach
- Lettuce
- Mushrooms
- Okra
- Onions
- Peppers
- Radishes
- Scallions
- Squash
- Tomato
- Turnip
- Zucchini

Other foods you can eat:

You can find a diverse range of foods; some of them are listed below:

- Seafood like shellfish, shrimp and crab
- Tofu
- Plant-based cheese and dairy products
- Avocados
- Nuts
- Coffee (unsweetened)
- Tea (unsweetened)
- Vegetable oil
- Cereal (unsweetened)
- Nutritious fruits like strawberries and apples

Food to Avoid

- Many foods are restricted, especially high carbohydrates containing foods. Except in fueling products, you should not consume any of the items listed below:
- Any type of fried food, including meat, vegetables and pastries
- Refined grains: White bread, white rice, pasta, biscuits, cakes, etc.
- High saturated fats: Butter, shortening (solid), coconut oil, etc.
- Whole fat dairy: Milk, cream, high-fat cheese, yogurt, etc.
- Sugary beverages: Juices, energy drinks, sodas, etc.

- Alcohol

Some foods are allowed in the 3&3 plan and not in 5&1. These are listed below:

- Fresh fruits
- Low-fat dairy
- Whole grains
- Legumes
- Starchy vegetables

How to Follow the Optavia Diet

The first thing you will do is call one of the Optivia coaches and set a diet plan. You will also tell your weight loss goals. After this conversation, you will then follow the 5&1 or 4&2&1 plan.

Initial stage:

In the 5&1 meal plan, you will eat six times a day, with one meal occurring every 2-3 hours. You will get 800-1000 calories and lose 5 kg or 12 pounds in 12 weeks. It is recommended for you to add 30 minutes of exercise, but this is not necessary.

You will buy Optavia fueling products on your coach's website, which are paid via commission.

If you opt for the slightly more flexible plan, you are then allowed a coach's approved snack such as celery sticks, half-cup of nuts, etc. The coaches provide a guide on how to order food and get lean and green meals for eating out.

Maintenance step:

Once you reach your goal weight, your daily calorie quota will increase to 1500 calories. You can now also add various more varieties of food such as vegetables and fruits. You are meant to be at this step for 6 weeks. Later on, you can apply to be an optavia couch yourself.

The Benefits of Optavia Diet

There are many benefits of this diet which are listed below:

Weight Loss:

Optavia is a meal replacement diet that reduces weight through portion control and decreasing calories and carbs. Many different types of studies show mixed results on whether meal replacement plans work better or worse than traditional calorie restriction plans. However, it is known that lowering calories and carbohydrate intake makes you lose weight. A 16-week study with almost 200 people showed that people on 5&1 plan Optavia lost much weight and had narrower waists. This can help prevent chronic diseases like diabetes and heart disease. The diet ensures quick weight loss, but many people regain weight after they stop.

It is convenient:

You are told what you have to eat and do not need to cook either. Lean green meals are easy to prepare. The coaches send you recipes and meal logs according to the instructions. You can replace lean and green meals with products such as 'flavors of home' and completely take cooking away.

No more hypertension:

Not Optavia diet specifically, but Medifast diet has been shown to reduce blood pressure in a study containing almost a hundred participants. The difference between Medifast and Optivia diet is that Optavia provides coaches. That is because the products are low in calories and sodium. You can also cut the salt in your meals to further decrease the amount.

FAQs

Question: What are the side effects?

Answer: Because of low calories, you can experience fatigue, cramps, headaches, dizziness, hair loss and menstrual changes.

Question: How much does it cost?

Answer: Signing up to the program and buying Medifast's fueling products can be expensive. The cost is around 500$ per three weeks.

Chapter 2: Air Fryer Basics

The air fryer is a cooking device that was invented in 2010. It is a small countertop kitchen appliance that looks like a convection oven. It cooks food using the process of hot air circulation with the use of a mechanical fan.

Even though it is called "air fryer", it can actually do more than just fry foods. It can also be used to sauté, stir fry, roast and even bake pastries and cakes.

Air Fryer Benefits

There are many benefits to using the air fryer. Here are some of those that you should definitely know about:

Benefit # 1 - Healthier Dishes

As it turns out, fried dishes can be healthy too, thanks to this amazing innovation known as the air fryer.
With this device, you can fry foods using just a little bit of oil, or even no oil at all.
You can cook French fries, breaded pork chops, fried chicken wings, onion rings and more.
The result is the same: golden fried dishes that are just as crispy and delicious as those that are fried using buckets of oil!

Benefit # 2 – Speed and Convenience

Everyone is busy these days.
Surely, anyone would be thankful for a cooking device that shaves off time and effort in food preparation.
This is exactly what the air fryer does.
When you fry dishes in a pan, you have to wait for the oil to heat up before you can start cooking. This takes valuable minutes. But with the air fryer, you can skip this process and get to the cooking right away.
Plus, the cooking process is much quicker. For example, you can cook perfectly golden potato fries within 15 minutes. If you used the oven, this will take you up to 45 minutes. The speedy cooking process spells convenience for you as this gives you more time to do other important tasks at home. And if you're in a hurry to get things done, this surely makes your workload easier.

Benefit # 3 – Versatility

The air fryer is more versatile than you realize.
As mentioned earlier, you can do a lot with it, other than just fry dishes.

You can also sauté, stir fry, broil, roast, grill and even bake pastries and cakes.

You can use this to create casseroles, grill meat and poultry, cook fish and seafood, make sandwiches, make desserts and many more.

You will be surprised at how varied the dishes that you can make with this simple cooking device.

It's quite small in size, but there are plenty available accessories that you can buy to create different kinds of dishes. Just a few of these are baking pans, cake pans, skewers, steamer basket and so on.

Benefit # 4 – Space Saver

This is something anyone with a small kitchen would surely appreciate.

The air fryer comes in a small compact size (even though it can do a lot of things!) that it can definitely help you save space in the kitchen countertop.

It is just the size of an average coffee maker so you don't have to worry about it taking too much space in your kitchen.

It's also easy to move and store.

Benefit # 5 – Simplicity

Some people are intimidated with other kitchen devices because they are complicated to use.

Even if you read the manual, you still won't understand how the device works. It takes quite some time before you can finally figure things out.

But with the air fryer, it's just as simple as choosing the cooking time and temperature. Even the recipes only require a few steps.

The process is not that elaborate that even beginners don't have any trouble using this kitchen device.

Benefit # 6 – Clean-up convenience

Let's face it, even though cooking is fun, cleaning up after is not.

This is another thing you'd love about the air fryer—you don't have to worry much about the cleanup.

The only parts you'll have to wash are the pan and basket. These are dishwasher safe. And because they have nonstick coated surface, the food does not stick, making cleanup very easy and convenient.

It will only take you a few minutes to get the cleaning done.

Benefit # 7 – Energy saver

When people think about electric cooking device, their first concern is their electric bill.

They want to avoid electric cooking appliances because many of these use up a lot of energy.

But with the air fryer, this shouldn't be a problem. This is an energy efficient cooking device that does not consume as much electricity as other electric appliances.

Keeping Your Device Clean

It's important to keep your air fryer clean so that you can be sure that the flavor from the dish that you cook today won't be transferred to the next dish that you'll cook.

To clean this device, you simply have to soak the basket, pan and tray in warm and soapy water for a few minutes. Wipe the inside and outside of the air fryer using a damp cloth. Make sure that you rinse and dry all parts thoroughly before you put them back into the device.

Never use any metal utensils such as fork for scraping off food particles as this will damage the nonstick coating of the device.

If there is any unpleasant smell, try removing it by cleaning the fryer with a mixture of baking soda and water.

It is essential to clean and maintain your air fryer regularly to keep it in good working condition.

Maintenance tips include:

- Checking to make sure that there is no food left behind after using the air fryer
- Freeing the air fryer from any foreign debris
- Checking all the parts including the pan, basket and try to ensure that there is no damage
- Storing the air fryer properly in clean and dry location when not in use

Tips for Success

Although they are similar, the parts of the air fryer can vary depending on the brand. This makes it imperative for you to read and understand the user manual before you start using this kitchen device.

There are three aspects of using the air fryer that you have to do correctly, and these include:

- Preparing the food
- Preparing the air fryer
- Cooking the dish

Tips for Food Preparation:

- Slice the food in equal portions

- Dry the food before seasoning with spices and herbs
- Spray oil on the basket or pan
- Follow the recipe carefully for preparing ingredients

Tips for Air Fryer Preparation:

- Make sure that the air fryer is clean
- Preheat the air fryer for at least 5 minutes

Tips for Cooking

- Follow the recipe instructions to the dot
- Shake the fryer once or twice to cook fried vegetables and other dishes evenly
- Open the air fryer to check if the food is cooking the right way

Now, let's get to know more about meal preparations.

Chapter 3: Breakfast

Tempeh

Preparation time: 5 minutes
Cooking time: 15 minutes
Servings: 4

Ingredients:

- 8 ounces tempeh, ½-inch cubed
- 1 teaspoon garlic powder
- ½ teaspoon sea salt
- 1 tablespoon soy sauce
- 1 tablespoon olive oil

Method:

1. Switch on the air fryer, insert fryer basket, grease it with non-stick cooking oil spray, then shut with its lid, set the fryer at 390 degrees F, and preheat for 5 minutes.
2. Meanwhile, place tempeh cubes in a large bowl, add remaining ingredients, toss until well combined and let it rest for 5 minutes.
3. Open the fryer, arrange tempeh cubes in the air fryer basket in a single layer, spray oil on the food, close with its lid and cook for 15 minutes until thoroughly cooked and nicely browned, turning halfway.
4. When the air fryer beeps, open its lid, take out the tempeh pieces and then serve.

Nutrition Value:

- Calories: 46 Cal
- Fat: 5 g
- Carbs: 1 g
- Protein: 1 g
- Fiber: 1 g

Egg White Muffins

Preparation time: 5 minutes
Cooking time: 30 minutes
Servings: 12

Ingredients:

- ½ cup diced bell peppers
- 1 cup baby spinach, chopped
- ½ cup diced baby tomatoes
- ½ teaspoon garlic powder
- ½ teaspoon salt
- ½ teaspoon ground black pepper
- 2 cups egg whites
- ½ cup cottage cheese

Method:

1. Switch on the air fryer, insert fryer basket, then shut with its lid, set the fryer at 400 degrees F, and preheat for 5 minutes.
2. Meanwhile, take a large bowl, place all the ingredients in it, whisk until combined and then divide this mixture evenly among 12 silicone muffin cups.
3. Open the fryer, arrange muffin cups in the air fryer basket in a single layer, close with its lid and cook for 12 to 15 minutes until thoroughly cooked.
4. When the air fryer beeps, open its lid, take out the muffin cups, cook the remaining muffins in the same manner and then serve.

Nutrition Value:

- Calories: 34 Cal
- Fat: 1 g
- Carbs: 1 g
- Protein: 6 g
- Fiber: 1 g

Broccoli Frittata

Preparation time: 5 minutes
Cooking time: 17 minutes
Servings: 4

Ingredients:

- ½ cup chopped broccoli florets
- ½ teaspoon salt
- ½ cup chopped bell pepper
- ¼ teaspoon ground black pepper
- 2 tablespoons almond milk, unsweetened
- 3 eggs
- 2 tablespoons grated parmesan cheese

Method:

1. Switch on the air fryer, insert fryer basket, then shut with its lid, set the fryer at 350 degrees F, and preheat for 5 minutes.
2. Meanwhile, take a heatproof dish, grease it with oil and then place bell peppers and florets in it.
3. Open the fryer, arrange the dish in the air fryer basket, close with its lid and cook for 7 minutes.
4. In the meantime, take a medium bowl, crack the eggs in it, add salt, black pepper and milk and then whisk until blended.
5. When the vegetables have cooked, pour the egg mixture over the vegetables, sprinkle cheese on top and then continue cooking for 10 minutes.
6. When the air fryer beeps, open its lid, take out the dish, cut frittata into slices and then serve.

Nutrition Value:

- Calories: 171 Cal
- Fat: 20.6 g
- Carbs: 5.6 g
- Protein: 16 g
- Fiber: 1.1 g

Sausages

Preparation time: 5 minutes
Cooking time: 12 minutes
Servings: 3

Ingredients:

- 6 Italian sausages

Method:

1. Switch on the air fryer, insert fryer basket, grease it with non-stick cooking oil spray, then shut with its lid, set the fryer at 400 degrees F, and preheat for 5 minutes.
2. Meanwhile, prepare the sausages and for this, poke each in three places with a knife.
3. Open the fryer, arrange sausages in the air fryer basket in a single layer, spray oil on the food, close with its lid and cook for 9 to 12 minutes until thoroughly cooked, turning halfway.
4. When the air fryer beeps, open its lid, take out the sausages and then serve.

Nutrition Value:

- Calories: 630 Cal
- Fat: 57 g
- Carbs: 1.2 g
- Protein: 25.9 g
- Fiber: 2 g

Sausage and Egg Breakfast Cups

Preparation time: 5 minutes
Cooking time: 40 minutes
Servings: 12

Ingredients:

- 1 pound sausage, ground
- 1 cup baby spinach
- 1 medium tomato, chopped
- ¼ teaspoon onion powder
- ¼ teaspoon garlic powder
- ½ teaspoon salt
- 1/3 teaspoon ground black pepper
- ¼ teaspoon paprika
- ¼ teaspoon dried parsley
- 6 eggs

Method:

1. Switch on the air fryer, insert fryer basket, then shut with its lid, set the fryer at 400 degrees F, and preheat for 5 minutes.
2. Meanwhile, take a large bowl, place all the ingredients in it, whisk until combined and then divide this mixture evenly among 12 silicone muffin cups.
3. Open the fryer, arrange muffin cups in the air fryer basket in a single layer, close with its lid and cook for 18 to 20 minutes until thoroughly cooked.
4. When the air fryer beeps, open its lid, take out the muffin cups, cook the remaining muffins in the same manner and then serve.

Nutrition Value:

- Calories: 155 Cal
- Fat: 12.6 g
- Carbs: 1.6 g
- Protein: 8.7 g
- Fiber: 0.2 g

Sausage Patties

Preparation time: 5 minutes
Cooking time: 8 minutes
Servings: 4

Ingredients:

- 12 ounces sausage patties, prepared

Method:

1. Switch on the air fryer, insert fryer basket, grease it with non-stick cooking oil spray, then shut with its lid, set the fryer at 400 degrees F, and preheat for 5 minutes.
2. Open the fryer, arrange sausage patties in the air fryer basket in a single layer, spray oil on the food, close with its lid and cook for 6 to 8 minutes until thoroughly cooked and nicely brown on all sides, turning halfway.
3. Serve straight away.

Nutrition Value:

- Calories: 145 Cal
- Fat: 9 g
- Carbs: 0.7 g
- Protein: 14.1 g
- Fiber: 1 g

Tofu Scramble

Preparation time: 5 minutes
Cooking time: 5 minutes
Servings: 3

Ingredients:

- 10 ounces tofu, extra-firm, pressed, drained
- ½ teaspoon salt
- 2 tablespoons paprika
- ½ teaspoon ground black pepper
- 1 tablespoon olive oil

Method:

1. Switch on the air fryer, insert fryer basket, then shut with its lid, set the fryer at 330 degrees F, and preheat for 5 minutes.
2. Meanwhile, place tofu in a bowl, add salt, black pepper and paprika and then mash with a fork until combined.
3. Take a heatproof dish that fits into the air fryer basket, grease it with oil and then spread tofu mixture in it in an even layer.
4. Open the fryer, place the prepared dish in the air fryer basket, close with its lid and cook for 10 minutes until thoroughly cooked and nicely browned, stirring halfway.
5. When the air fryer beeps, open its lid, take out the dish and then serve.

Nutrition Value:

- Calories: 144 Cal
- Fat: 10.4 g
- Carbs: 5.3 g
- Protein: 4.7 g
- Fiber: 1.5 g

Crustless Mini Taco Quiche

Preparation time: 10 minutes
Cooking time: 28 minutes
Servings: 4

Ingredients:

- 1 medium green bell pepper, cored, diced
- ½ pound ground pork
- 1 small red onion, peeled, diced
- ½ pound ground beef
- 1 medium red bell pepper, cored, diced
- 1 teaspoon salt
- 2 tablespoons taco seasoning
- 1 teaspoon ground black pepper
- ¼ cup tomato salsa
- ¼ cup vegan heavy cream
- 4 eggs
- 1 cup shredded Mexican blend cheese

Method:

1. Take a medium skillet pan, place it over medium-high heat and when hot, add ground pork and beef.
2. Stir in salt and black pepper, and then cook the meat for 8 to 10 minutes until nicely browned.
3. Add onion and bell peppers, stir in taco seasoning and continue cooking the meat for 4 minutes until vegetables turn soft.
4. Meanwhile, take a large bowl, crack the eggs in it, add salsa, cream and cheese and then whisk until well combined.
5. Take four mini pie pans, grease them with oil, evenly fill the pans with the cooked meat mixture and then cover with the egg mixture.
6. Switch on the air fryer, insert fryer basket, then shut with its lid, set the fryer at 350 degrees F, and preheat for 5 minutes.
7. Open the fryer, arrange pie pans in the air fryer basket in a single layer, close with its lid and cook for 12 minutes until thoroughly cooked.
8. Serve straight away.

Nutrition Value:

- Calories: 100 Cal
- Fat: 100 g
- Carbs: 100 g
- Protein: 100 g
- Fiber: 100 g

Lentil Sliders

Preparation time: 5 minutes
Cooking time: 20 minutes
Servings: 8

Ingredients:

- 2 cups cooked lentils
- 1 teaspoon salt
- 1 cup vegan seasoned croutons
- 1 teaspoon ground black pepper
- 1 tablespoon olive oil
- ½ cup almond milk, unsweetened

Method:

1. Switch on the air fryer, insert fryer basket, layer it with foil, grease it with non-stick cooking oil spray, then shut with its lid, set the fryer at 350 degrees F, and preheat for 5 minutes.
2. Meanwhile, place cooked lentils in a food processor, add croutons and then pulse until well combined.
3. Add remaining ingredients, pulse until thoroughly cooked, shape the mixture into evenly sized eight portions and then shape each portion into a ball.
4. Open the fryer, arrange prepared lentil balls in the air fryer basket in a single layer, spray oil on the food, close with its lid and cook for 8 to 10 minutes until thoroughly cooked and golden brown, turning halfway.
5. Serve straight away.

Nutrition Value:

- Calories: 127.6 Cal
- Fat: 1.5 g
- Carbs: 24.2 g
- Protein: 5.2 g
- Fiber: 4.8 g

Oatmeal Muffins

Preparation time: 5 minutes
Cooking time: 12 minutes
Servings: 6

Ingredients:

- 2 cups rolled oats, old-fashioned
- 1 ½ cup almond flour
- 1 teaspoon ground cinnamon
- 2/3 cup coconut sugar
- 1 teaspoon baking powder
- 1 teaspoon salt
- ½ teaspoon baking soda
- ½ cup agave syrup
- 1 cup oat milk
- 2 eggs
- 1/3 cup olive oil

Method:

1. Switch on the air fryer, insert fryer basket, then shut with its lid, set the fryer at 320 degrees F, and preheat for 5 minutes.
2. Meanwhile, take a large bowl, place all the ingredients in it and then whisk until well combined and smooth batter comes together.
3. Take six silicone muffin cups, grease them with oil and then evenly fill them with the prepared batter.
4. Open the fryer, arrange prepared muffin cups in the air fryer basket in a single layer, close with its lid and cook for 12 minutes until thoroughly cooked and the top turn golden.
5. Serve straight away.

Nutrition Value:

- Calories: 143.8 Cal
- Fat: 4.1 g
- Carbs: 27.4 g
- Protein: 3.8 g
- Fiber: 1.5 g

Muffinless Egg Cups

Preparation time: 5 minutes
Cooking time: 30 minutes
Servings: 12

Ingredients:

- 12 pieces of bacon
- ¼ cup chopped green chilies
- 1 cup spinach leaves
- 1/8 teaspoon salt
- 8 egg whites
- ½ teaspoon ground black pepper
- 4 eggs

Method:

1. Switch on the air fryer, insert fryer basket, then shut with its lid, set the fryer at 375 degrees F, and preheat for 5 minutes.
2. Meanwhile, take a large bowl, place all the ingredients in it except for bacon and then whisk until combined.
3. Take twelve silicone muffin cups, line each muffin cup with a bacon slice and then evenly fill with the blended mixture.
4. Open the fryer, arrange muffin cups in the air fryer basket in a single layer, close with its lid and cook for 13 to 15 minutes until thoroughly cooked.
5. When the air fryer beeps, open its lid, take out the muffin cups, cook the remaining muffins in the same manner and then serve.

Nutrition Value:

- Calories: 163 Cal
- Fat: 6.5 g
- Carbs: 3.4 g
- Protein: 22 g
- Fiber: 1 g

Egg White Muffin Cups with Peppers

Preparation time: 5 minutes
Cooking time: 40 minutes
Servings: 12

Ingredients:

- 8 sweet bell peppers, small size, cored, diced
- 10 slices of bacon, diced
- 1/3 teaspoon salt
- ¼ teaspoon ground black pepper
- ¼ teaspoon dried thyme
- 2 cups egg whites

Method:

1. Switch on the air fryer, insert fryer basket, then shut with its lid, set the fryer at 400 degrees F, and preheat for 5 minutes.
2. Meanwhile, take a large bowl, place all the ingredients in it, whisk until combined and then divide this mixture evenly among 12 silicone muffin cups.
3. Open the fryer, arrange muffin cups in the air fryer basket in a single layer, close with its lid and cook for 18 to 20 minutes until thoroughly cooked.
4. When the air fryer beeps, open its lid, take out the muffin cups, cook the remaining muffins in the same manner and then serve.

Nutrition Value:

- Calories: 50 Cal
- Fat: 2 g
- Carbs: 3 g
- Protein: 4 g
- Fiber: 1 g

Tofu Spinach Sauté

Preparation time: 5 minutes
Cooking time: 15 minutes
Servings: 2

Ingredients:

- 8 ounces tofu, extra-firm, pressed, cubed
- ¼ cup chopped onion
- 4 cups baby spinach
- ¼ cup chopped mushrooms
- 4 grape tomatoes, chopped
- 3 teaspoons nutritional yeast
- 1 teaspoon soy sauce

Method:

1. Switch on the air fryer, insert fryer basket, place a heatproof dish in it, grease it with oil, then shut with its lid, set the fryer at 400 degrees F, and preheat for 5 minutes.
2. Then open the fryer, add onion and mushrooms into the dish, spray with some oil, close with its lid and cook for 4 to 5 minutes until vegetables have turned soft.
3. Add tofu, toss until combined, continue cooking for 2 to 3 minutes and then stir in soy sauce and nutritional yeast.
4. Add chopped tomatoes and spinach, continue cooking for 4 to 6 minutes until spinach leaves begin to wilt.
5. Serve straight away.

Nutrition Value:

- Calories: 202 Cal
- Fat: 11 g
- Carbs: 7 g
- Protein: 18 g
- Fiber: 5 g

Spinach Frittata

Preparation time: 5 minutes
Cooking time: 10 minutes
Servings: 4

Ingredients:

- 1 green onion, chopped
- ½ cup spinach leaves
- 2 tablespoons diced red bell pepper
- 1/8 teaspoon cayenne pepper
- 4 eggs
- ½ cup shredded cheese

Method:

1. Switch on the air fryer, insert fryer basket, grease it with non-stick cooking oil spray, then shut with its lid, set the fryer at 390 degrees F, and preheat for 5 minutes.
2. Meanwhile, take a large bowl, place all the ingredients in it, whisk until combined and then spoon the mixture into a heatproof dish greased with oil.
3. Open the fryer, arrange the prepared dish in the air fryer basket, close with its lid and cook for 10 minutes until thoroughly cooked.
4. Serve straight away.

Nutrition Value:

- Calories: 194 Cal
- Fat: 11.2 g
- Carbs: 4.1 g
- Protein: 12.8 g
- Fiber: 1.4 g

Chocolate Chip and Oatmeal Cookies

Preparation time: 5 minutes
Cooking time: 40 minutes
Servings: 36

Ingredients:

- ¾ cup almond flour
- 1 ½ cups oats, quick-cooking
- ¾ cup coconut sugar
- ½ teaspoon salt
- ½ teaspoon baking soda
- 1 cup chocolate chips, semisweet
- 1.7 ounces vanilla pudding mix
- ½ cup coconut butter, softened
- ½ teaspoon vanilla extract, unsweetened
- ½ cup chopped nuts
- 1 egg

Method:

1. Switch on the air fryer, insert fryer basket, grease it with non-stick cooking oil spray, then shut with its lid, set the fryer at 325 degrees F, and preheat for 5 minutes.
2. Meanwhile, take a large bowl, place butter in it, beat in sugar until creamy and then beat in vanilla and egg until smooth.
3. Take a separate bowl, place almond flour in it, add oats, pudding mix, salt and baking soda and then stir until combined.
4. Whisk the oat mixture into the egg mixture until incorporated, and then stir in nuts and chocolate chips until incorporated.
5. Take a large baking sheet, grease it with oil, scoop the batter, and then flatten slightly into a cookie.
6. Open the fryer, arrange cookies in the air fryer basket in a single layer, close with its lid and cook for 8 to 10 minutes until thoroughly cooked and golden.
7. Cook remaining cookies in the same manner and then serve.

Nutrition Value:

- Calories: 102 Cal
- Fat: 5 g
- Carbs: 13 g
- Protein: 2 g
- Fiber: 1 g

Chapter 4: Lean & Green Poultry

Crustless Chicken and Spinach Quiche

Preparation time: 10 minutes
Cooking time: 40 minutes
Servings: 3

Ingredients:

- 1 ½ cups shredded cooked chicken
- 5 ounces spinach, chopped
- 1 1/2 cups chopped mushrooms
- 3 tablespoons chopped onion
- 1 teaspoon sea salt
- 6 eggs
- 1 ½ cups vegan heavy cream
- 1 teaspoon ground black pepper
- 1 ½ cups vegan grated cheddar cheese
- 1 ½ cups vegan ricotta cheese

Method:

1. Switch on the air fryer, insert fryer basket, then shut with its lid, set the fryer at 375 degrees F, and preheat for 5 minutes.
2. Meanwhile, take a heatproof bowl, place spinach in it, drizzle with 1 tablespoon water and then microwave at the high heat setting for 1 to 2 minutes until spinach leaves wilt.
3. Drain the spinach and then chop it.
4. Take a large bowl, crack the eggs in it, add spinach and remaining ingredients and then stir until well combined.
5. Take three mini pie pans that fit into the air fryer basket, grease them with oil and then evenly spoon the prepared mixture in it.
6. Open the fryer, arrange a prepared pie pan in the air fryer basket, close with its lid and cook for 10 to 15 minutes until thoroughly cooked and the top turned golden brown, turning halfway.
7. Serve straight away.

Nutrition Value:

- Calories: 398 Cal
- Fat: 34 g
- Carbs: 5 g
- Protein: 18 g
- Fiber: 1 g

Crispy Chicken Dinner

Preparation time: 15 minutes
Cooking time: 16 minutes
Servings: 4

Ingredients:

- 4 chicken breasts, , each about 8 ounces, pounded
- ½ cup oats
- ¼ teaspoon salt and more as needed
- ¼ teaspoon ground black pepper and more as needed
- 1 cup buttermilk
- ¾ cup vegan cheese blend

Method:

1. Take a large bowl, place chicken breasts in it, pour in the milk, season with some salt and black pepper, toss until combined and then let the chicken marinate for 10 minutes.
2. Switch on the air fryer, insert fryer basket, grease it with non-stick cooking oil spray, then shut with its lid, set the fryer at 400 degrees F, and preheat for 5 minutes.
3. Meanwhile, take a shallow dish, place oats in it, and then stir in salt, black pepper, and cheese.
4. When the chicken has marinated, dredge it into oats mixture until well coated.
5. Open the fryer, arrange chicken breasts in the air fryer basket in a single layer, spray oil on the food, close with its lid and cook for 8 minutes until thoroughly cooked and golden brown, turning halfway.
6. Serve straight away.

Nutrition Value:

- Calories: 570 Cal
- Fat: 16 g
- Carbs: 49 g
- Protein: 55 g
- Fiber: 3 g

Breaded Chicken Breasts

Preparation time: 10 minutes
Cooking time: 22 minutes
Servings: 4

Ingredients:

- 1 pound chicken breast, skinless, pounded
- 1 teaspoon salt
- 1 cup oats
- 1 teaspoon ground black pepper
- 1 cup almond flour
- 1 egg

Method:

1. Switch on the air fryer, insert fryer basket, grease it with non-stick cooking oil spray, then shut with its lid, set the fryer at 390 degrees F, and preheat for 5 minutes.
2. Meanwhile, take a shallow dish, place flour in it, add ½ teaspoon each of salt and black pepper and then stir until mixed.
3. Take a medium bowl, crack the egg in it and then whisk until blended.
4. Take a separate shallow dish, place oats in it, add remaining salt and black pepper and then stir until mixed.
5. Working on each chicken breast at a time, dredge into the almond flour mixture, dip into the egg and then dredge into the oats mixture until coated.
6. Open the fryer, arrange the prepared chicken breasts in the air fryer basket in a single layer, spray oil on the food, close with its lid and cook for 22 minutes until thoroughly cooked, turning halfway.
7. Serve straight away.

Nutrition Value:

- Calories: 393 Cal
- Fat: 5.1 g
- Carbs: 49.2 g
- Protein: 34.5 g
- Fiber: 0.2 g

Ranch Chicken Tenders

Preparation time: 10 minutes
Cooking time: 25 minutes
Servings: 8

Ingredients:

- 14 ounces chicken tenders, skinless
- 2 tablespoons almond flour
- 2/3 cup oats
- ¼ teaspoon salt
- 2 teaspoons chicken seasoning
- ¼ teaspoon ground black pepper
- 1/3 cup ranch dressing
- ½ cup vegan shredded cheddar cheese

Method:

1. Switch on the air fryer, insert fryer basket, line it with parchment sheet, grease it with non-stick cooking oil spray, then shut with its lid, set the fryer at 325 degrees F, and preheat for 5 minutes.
2. Meanwhile, take a shallow dish, almond flour in it, add chicken seasoning and then stir until combined.
3. Take a separate shallow dish, oats in it, add salt and black pepper and then stir until combined.
4. Take a separate shallow dish and then place the ranch dressing in it.
5. Working on one chicken tender at a time, dredge it in almond flour mixture, dip into the ranch dressing
6. and dredge into the oat mixture until well-coated.
7. Open the fryer, arrange chicken tenders in the air fryer basket in a single layer, spray oil on the food, close with its lid and cook for 20 to 25 minutes until thoroughly cooked and golden brown, turning halfway.
8. Serve straight away.

Nutrition Value:

- Calories: 150 Cal
- Fat: 7 g
- Carbs: 9 g
- Protein: 13 g
- Fiber: 2 g

Chicken Nuggets

Preparation time: 5 minutes
Cooking time: 30 minutes
Servings: 4

Ingredients:

- 1 chicken breast, about 8 ounces, boneless, skinless
- ½ cup coconut butter, melted
- ¼ teaspoon salt
- ½ cup oats
- 1/8 teaspoon ground black pepper

Method:

1. Switch on the air fryer, insert fryer basket, grease it with non-stick cooking oil spray, then shut with its lid, set the fryer at 390 degrees F, and preheat for 5 minutes.
2. Meanwhile, cut the chicken breast into ½-inch thick slices and then season with salt and black pepper.
3. Take a small heatproof bowl, place butter in it and then microwave at the high heat setting until melted.
4. Take a shallow dish and then place oats in it.
5. Working on each chicken piece at a time, dip into the melted butter and then dredge in oats until coated.
6. Open the fryer, arrange the prepared chicken nuggets in the air fryer basket in a single layer, spray oil on the food, close with its lid and cook for 8 minutes until thoroughly cooked and golden brown, turning halfway.
7. Serve straight away.

Nutrition Value:

- Calories: 190 Cal
- Fat: 8.7 g
- Carbs: 19.5 g
- Protein: 7.7 g
- Fiber: 1.2 g

Garlic Chicken Tenders

Preparation time: 5 minutes
Cooking time: 25 minutes
Servings: 4

Ingredients:

- 8 chicken tenders, skinless
- 2 tablespoons water

- 1 egg

For the Coating:

- 1 cup oats
- ½ teaspoon onion powder
- 1 teaspoon garlic powder

- ¼ teaspoon ground black pepper
- ½ teaspoon salt
- ¼ cup vegan parmesan cheese

Method:

1. Switch on the air fryer, insert fryer basket, line it with parchment sheet, grease it with non-stick cooking oil spray, then shut with its lid, set the fryer at 400 degrees F, and preheat for 5 minutes.
2. Meanwhile, take a shallow dish, place all the ingredients for the coating
3. and then stir until combined.
4. Take a separate shallow dish, crack the egg in it, add water, and whisk until blended.
5. Working on one chicken tender at a time, dip into the egg and then dredge into the oat mixture until well coated.
6. Open the fryer, arrange chicken tenders in the air fryer basket in a single layer, spray oil on the food, close with its lid and cook for 12 minutes until thoroughly cooked and golden brown, turning halfway.
7. Serve straight away.

Nutrition Value:

- Calories: 220 Cal
- Fat: 6 g
- Carbs: 13 g

- Protein: 27 g
- Fiber: 1 g

Turkey Breast

Preparation time: 10 minutes
Cooking time: 50 minutes
Servings: 4

Ingredients:

- 2 pounds turkey breasts, skin-on, bone-in
- 1 tablespoon olive oil
- 1 teaspoon seasoning salt

Method:

1. Switch on the air fryer, insert fryer basket, grease it with non-stick cooking oil spray, then shut with its lid, set the fryer at 350 degrees F, and preheat for 5 minutes.
2. Meanwhile, prepare the turkey breasts and for this, rub them with oil and then season with seasoning salt.
3. Open the fryer, arrange turkey breasts skin-side-down in the air fryer basket in a single layer, spray oil on the food, close with its lid and cook for 50 minutes until thoroughly cooked, turning halfway.
4. Serve straight away.

Nutrition Value:

- Calories: 97 Cal
- Fat: 3 g
- Carbs: 1 g
- Protein: 17 g
- Fiber: 0 g

Chicken Cauliflower Fried Rice

Preparation time: 5 minutes
Cooking time: 12 minutes
Servings: 4

Ingredients:

- 24 ounces frozen cauliflower rice
- 1 cup shredded cooked chicken
- ½ cup chopped green onions
- ½ teaspoon salt
- ¼ cup soy sauce
- 4 eggs

Method:

1. Switch on the air fryer, insert fryer basket, line the bottom with foil about ½-inch along the sides, then shut with its lid, set the fryer at 400 degrees F, and preheat for 5 minutes.
2. Meanwhile, take a heatproof bowl, place cauliflower rice in it and then microwave for 5 minutes.
3. Add remaining ingredients to the cauliflower rice and then stir until well combined.
4. Spoon the cauliflower mixture into the fryer basket, spray oil on the food, close with its lid and cook for 10 to 12 minutes until thoroughly cooked, stirring halfway.
5. Serve straight away.

Nutrition Value:

- Calories: 170 Cal
- Fat: 7.4 g
- Carbs: 11.6 g
- Protein: 16.2 g
- Fiber: 4.8 g

Tender Chicken Breasts

Preparation time: 10 minutes
Cooking time: 22 minutes
Servings: 4

Ingredients:

- 4 chicken breasts, each about 8 ounces, boneless, skinless
- ½ teaspoon garlic powder
- 1/8 teaspoon ground black pepper
- ½ teaspoon salt
- ½ teaspoon dried oregano
- 2 tablespoons olive oil

Method:

1. Switch on the air fryer, insert fryer basket, grease it with non-stick cooking oil spray, then shut with its lid, set the fryer at 360 degrees F, and preheat for 5 minutes.
2. Meanwhile, take a small bowl, place garlic powder, salt, black pepper and oregano and then stir until well combined.
3. Brush oil on both sides of the chicken and then season with the spice mix until coated.
4. Open the fryer, arrange the prepared chicken breasts in the air fryer basket in a single layer, close with its lid and cook for 20 to 22 minutes until thoroughly cooked and golden brown, turning halfway.
5. Serve straight away.

Nutrition Value:

- Calories: 163 Cal
- Fat: 3 g
- Carbs: 1 g
- Protein: 30 g
- Fiber: 0.4 g

Chicken and Vegetables Fried Rice

Preparation time: 5 minutes
Cooking time: 25 minutes
Servings: 6

Ingredients:

- 1 cup leftover chicken, cut into cubes
- 1 ½ cup frozen vegetables
- 4 cups cauliflower rice
- 2 green onions, sliced
- 1 teaspoon salt
- 1 tablespoon red chili sauce
- 5 tablespoons soy sauce
- 2 teaspoons olive oil

Method:

1. Switch on the air fryer, insert fryer basket, then shut with its lid, set the fryer at 350 degrees F, and preheat for 5 minutes.
2. Meanwhile, take a large bowl, place all the ingredients in it and then stir until well combined.
3. Take a large heatproof pan that could fit in the air fryer basket and then spoon rice mixture in it.
4. Open the fryer, place the prepared pan in the air fryer basket, spray oil on the food, close with its lid and cook for 20 to 25 minutes until thoroughly cooked, stirring halfway.
5. Serve straight away.

Nutrition Value:

- Calories: 220 Cal
- Fat: 1 g
- Carbs: 40 g
- Protein: 15 g
- Fiber: 3 g

Turkey Burgers

Preparation time: 10 minutes
Cooking time: 20 minutes
Servings: 4

Ingredients:

- 1 pound ground turkey
- 1/3 cup oats
- ½ teaspoon onion powder
- 1 teaspoon salt
- 1 teaspoon garlic powder
- ½ teaspoon ground black pepper
- ¼ teaspoon poultry seasoning
- 1 egg
- ¼ cup almond milk, unsweetened

Method:

1. Switch on the air fryer, insert fryer basket, grease it with non-stick cooking oil spray, then shut with its lid, set the fryer at 360 degrees F, and preheat for 5 minutes.
2. Meanwhile, crack the egg in a medium bowl, add oats, pour in the milk and then stir until well mixed.
3. Add onion powder, salt, garlic powder, black pepper and poultry seasoning
4. stir until mixed and then stir in ground turkey until well combined.
5. Shape the mixture into four portions and then shape each portion into a patty.
6. Open the fryer, arrange prepared turkey patties in the air fryer basket in a single layer, spray oil on the food, close with its lid and cook for 15 to 20 minutes until thoroughly cooked and golden brown, turning halfway.
7. Serve straight away.

Nutrition Value:

- Calories: 148 Cal
- Fat: 3 g
- Carbs: 2 g
- Protein: 28 g
- Fiber: 0.6 g

Cornish Hens

Servings: 4
Preparation time: 10 minutes
Cooking time: 1 hour and 30 minutes

Ingredients:

- 2 Cornish game hens
- ½ teaspoon dried thyme
- 1 teaspoon garlic powder
- ½ teaspoon dried oregano
- 1 tablespoon salt
- 1 teaspoon smoked paprika
- 1 teaspoon ground black pepper
- ½ teaspoon dried basil
- 2 tablespoons olive oil

Method:

1. Switch on the air fryer, insert fryer basket, grease it with non-stick cooking oil spray, then shut with its lid, set the fryer at 390 degrees F, and preheat for 5 minutes.
2. Meanwhile, take a small bowl, place oil in it, add all the seasonings, stir until combined and then rub this mixture all over the game hens until well coated.
3. Open the fryer, arrange a game hen in the air fryer basket, close with its lid and cook for 45 minutes until thoroughly cooked and golden brown, turning halfway.
4. Cook the remaining game hen in the same manner, cut into pieces and then serve.

Nutrition Value:

- Calories: 400 Cal
- Fat: 31 g
- Carbs: 1 g
- Protein: 29 g
- Fiber: 0.2 g

Hasselback Fajita Chicken

Preparation time: 10 minutes
Cooking time: 30 minutes
Servings: 4

Ingredients:

- ½ of medium orange bell pepper, cored, sliced
- 4 chicken breasts, each about 8 ounces, boneless, skinless
- ½ of medium red bell pepper, cored, sliced
- 1 medium red onion, peeled, sliced
- ½ of medium yellow bell pepper, cored, sliced
- 2 tablespoons fajita seasoning
- ½ cup vegan shredded cheese mix
- 2 tablespoons olive oil
- 2 tablespoons chopped cilantro

Method:

1. Switch on the air fryer, insert fryer basket, grease it with non-stick cooking oil spray, then shut with its lid, set the fryer at 380 degrees F, and preheat for 5 minutes.
2. Meanwhile, prepare the chicken breasts and for this, make horizontal cuts into each chicken and then brush with oil.
3. Season the chicken breasts with fajita seasoning until well coated, and then place onion and bell peppers pieces into each cut.
4. Open the fryer, arrange prepared chicken breasts in the air fryer basket in a single layer, spray oil on the food, close with its lid and cook for 15 minutes until thoroughly cooked.
5. Sprinkle cheese over the chicken breasts and then continue cooking for 2 to 3 minutes until cheese has melted and turned golden.
6. Sprinkle cilantro over the chicken breasts and then serve.

Nutrition Value:

- Calories: 368 Cal
- Fat: 11 g
- Carbs: 9 g
- Protein: 53 g
- Fiber: 1 g

Venison Burgers

Preparation time: 10 minutes
Cooking time: 10 minutes
Servings: 4

Ingredients:

- 1 pound ground venison
- ½ teaspoon onion powder
- 1 teaspoon seasoned salt
- ½ teaspoon ground black pepper
- 2 teaspoons Worcestershire sauce

Method:

1. Switch on the air fryer, insert fryer basket, grease it with non-stick cooking oil spray, then shut with its lid, set the fryer at 400 degrees F, and preheat for 5 minutes.
2. Meanwhile, take a large bowl, place all the ingredients in it, stir until combined and then shape the mixture into four evenly sized patties.
3. Open the fryer, arrange venison burgers in the air fryer basket in a single layer, spray oil on the food, close with its lid and cook for 8 to 10 minutes until thoroughly cooked and golden brown, turning halfway.
4. Serve straight away.

Nutrition Value:

- Calories: 247.3 Cal
- Fat: 4.5 g
- Carbs: 22.5 g
- Protein: 27.2 g
- Fiber: 1 g

Buttermilk Chicken

Preparation time: 10 minutes
Cooking time: 15 minutes
Servings: 6

Ingredients:

- 1 ½ pound boneless, skinless chicken thighs
- 1 cup oats
- 1 cup almond flour
- ½ tablespoon ground black pepper
- 1 tablespoon seasoned salt
- 2 cups buttermilk

Method:

1. Take a large bowl, place chicken thighs in it, add buttermilk and then let the chicken rest in the refrigerator for a minimum of 4 hours.
2. Then switch on the air fryer, insert fryer basket, grease it with non-stick cooking oil spray, then shut with its lid, set the fryer at 380 degrees F, and preheat for 5 minutes.
3. Meanwhile, take a large plastic bag
4. place almond flour in it, add salt and black pepper and then add chicken thighs.
5. Seal the bag and then turn it upside down until chicken thighs are coated in flour.
6. Take a shallow dish and then place oats in it.
7. Working on chicken thigh at a time, dip into buttermilk and then dredge in oats until well coated.
8. Open the fryer, arrange prepared chicken thighs in the air fryer basket in a single layer, spray oil on the food, close with its lid and cook for 15 minutes until thoroughly cooked and golden brown, turning halfway.
9. Serve straight away.

Nutrition Value:

- Calories: 335 Cal
- Fat: 12.8 g
- Carbs: 33.2 g
- Protein: 24.5 g
- Fiber: 0.8 g

Roast Duck

Preparation time: 10 minutes
Cooking time: 40 minutes
Servings: 4

Ingredients:

- 5 pounds whole duck, cleaned
- 2 teaspoons salt
- 1 tablespoon dried thyme
- 2 teaspoons ground black pepper
- 3 tablespoons olive oil

Method:

1. Switch on the air fryer, insert fryer basket, grease it with non-stick cooking oil spray, then shut with its lid, set the fryer at 365 degrees F, and preheat for 5 minutes.
2. Meanwhile, rub the duck with oil and then season with salt, thyme and black pepper until well coated.
3. Open the fryer, arrange the prepared duck in the air fryer basket, close with its lid and cook for 40 minutes until thoroughly cooked and golden brown, turning halfway.
4. When done, cut the duck into slices and then serve.

Nutrition Value:

- Calories: 1137 Cal
- Fat: 110 g
- Carbs: 3 g
- Protein: 33 g
- Fiber: 1 g

Naked Chicken Tenders

Preparation time: 5 minutes
Cooking time: 15 minutes
Servings: 4

Ingredients:

- 6 chicken tenders, skinless
- 1 teaspoon garlic powder
- 1 teaspoon salt
- 1 teaspoon onion powder
- 1 teaspoon dried oregano
- 1 teaspoon paprika

Method:

1. Switch on the air fryer, insert fryer basket, grease it with non-stick cooking oil spray, then shut with its lid, set the fryer at 380 degrees F, and preheat for 5 minutes.
2. Meanwhile, take a resealable plastic bag
3. place chicken tenders in it and then add the remaining ingredients.
4. Seal the bag and then turn it upside down until chicken tenders are coated in the seasonings.
5. Open the fryer, arrange the chicken tenders in the air fryer basket in a single layer, spray oil on the food, close with its lid and cook for 13 to 15 minutes until thoroughly cooked and golden brown, turning halfway.
6. Serve straight away.

Nutrition Value:

- Calories: 200 Cal
- Fat: 4 g
- Carbs: 12.9 g
- Protein: 27.7 g
- Fiber: 2.3 g

Chicken Wings

Preparation time: 10 minutes
Cooking time: 16 minutes
Servings: 4

Ingredients:

- 1 pound chicken wings
- 1 teaspoon garlic powder
- ¼ teaspoon salt
- ¼ teaspoon paprika
- ¼ teaspoon ground black pepper
- 2 tablespoons olive oil

Method:

1. Switch on the air fryer, insert fryer basket, grease it with non-stick cooking oil spray, then shut with its lid, set the fryer at 400 degrees F, and preheat for 5 minutes.
2. Meanwhile, take a medium bowl, place chicken wings in it, add remaining ingredients and then stir until well combined.
3. Open the fryer, arrange chicken wings in the air fryer basket in a single layer, spray oil on the food, close with its lid and cook for 8 minutes until thoroughly cooked and golden brown, turning halfway.
4. Serve straight away.

Nutrition Value:

- Calories: 234 Cal
- Fat: 17 g
- Carbs: 10 g
- Protein: 11 g
- Fiber: 1 g

Cracklin' Chicken

Preparation time: 10 minutes
Cooking time: 18 minutes
Servings: 4

Ingredients:

- 1.25 pounds chicken thighs, skin-on, bone-in
- 1 teaspoon salt
- ½ teaspoon seasoning salt

Method:

1. Switch on the air fryer, insert fryer basket, grease it with non-stick cooking oil spray, then shut with its lid, set the fryer at 400 degrees F, and preheat for 5 minutes.
2. Meanwhile, pound the chicken thighs and then sprinkle with salt and seasoning salt until coated.
3. Open the fryer, arrange the chicken thighs in the air fryer basket in a single layer, spray oil on the food, close with its lid and cook for 15 to 18 minutes until thoroughly cooked, turning halfway.
4. Serve straight away.

Nutrition Value:

- Calories: 371 Cal
- Fat: 28 g
- Carbs: 1 g
- Protein: 28 g
- Fiber: 0.3 g

Venison Bites

Preparation time: 10 minutes
Cooking time: 10 minutes
Servings: 6

Ingredients:

- 1 pound venison tenderloin, cut into bite-sized pieces
- 1 teaspoon onion powder
- ½ tablespoon ground cumin
- 1 teaspoon garlic powder
- 3 tablespoons Worcestershire sauce
- ½ teaspoon ground black pepper
- 1 teaspoon balsamic vinegar
- 3 tablespoons agave syrup
- ½ teaspoon vanilla extract, unsweetened
- 1 tablespoon liquid smoke
- 1 tablespoon olive oil

Method:

1. Take a large bowl and then place venison steak pieces in it.
2. Take a small bowl, place remaining ingredients in it, stir until combined and then drizzle the mixture over the steak pieces.
3. Toss until combined, cover the bowl with its lid and then let the venison marinate for 1 hour in the refrigerator.
4. Switch on the air fryer, insert fryer basket, grease it with non-stick cooking oil spray, then shut with its lid, set the fryer at 400 degrees F, and preheat for 5 minutes.
5. Open the fryer, arrange the venison steak pieces in the air fryer basket in a single layer, close with its lid and cook for 10 minutes until thoroughly cooked, turning halfway.
6. Serve straight away.

Nutrition Value:

- Calories: 156 Cal
- Fat: 4 g
- Carbs: 12 g
- Protein: 18 g
- Fiber: 2 g

Chapter 5: Lean & Green Pork

Spiced Pork Chops with Broccoli

Preparation time: 10 minutes
Cooking time: 12 minutes
Servings: 2

Ingredients:

- 2 pork chops, bone-in, each about 5 ounces
- 2 cups broccoli florets
- 1 teaspoon minced garlic
- ½ teaspoon onion powder
- 1 teaspoon salt, divided
- ½ teaspoon garlic powder
- ½ teaspoon paprika
- 2 tablespoons olive oil, divided

Method:

1. Switch on the air fryer, insert fryer basket, grease it with non-stick cooking oil spray, then shut with its lid, set the fryer at 350 degrees F, and preheat for 5 minutes.
2. Meanwhile, take a small bowl, place ½ teaspoon salt, garlic powder, onion powder and paprika and then stir until mixed.
3. Rub the pork chops with oil and then sprinkle with the spice mix until well coated.
4. Open the fryer, arrange pork chops in the air fryer basket in a single layer, spray oil on the food, close with its lid and cook for 7 minutes until thoroughly cooked and golden brown, turning halfway.
5. Meanwhile, take a large bowl, place broccoli florets in it, add minced garlic and remaining salt and oil and then toss until coated.
6. After 7 minutes of cooking time, turn the pork chops, add broccoli florets and then continue cooking for 5 minutes.
7. Serve straight away.

Nutrition Value:

- Calories: 483 Cal
- Fat: 30 g
- Carbs: 12 g
- Protein: 40 g
- Fiber: 6 g

Pork Loin

Preparation time: 10 minutes
Cooking time: 25 minutes
Servings: 6

Ingredients:

- 1.5-pound pork tenderloin
- 1 ½ teaspoon salt
- 1 tablespoon minced garlic
- 1 teaspoon ground black pepper
- 2 tablespoons olive oil

Method:

1. Switch on the air fryer, insert fryer basket, grease it with non-stick cooking oil spray, then shut with its lid, set the fryer at 390 degrees F, and preheat for 5 minutes.
2. Meanwhile, coat with oil, rub with garlic and then season with salt and black pepper.
3. Open the fryer, arrange pork tenderloin in the air fryer basket in a single layer, close with its lid and cook for 25 minutes until thoroughly cooked and golden brown, turning halfway.
4. Serve straight away.

Nutrition Value:

- Calories: 379 Cal
- Fat: 10 g
- Carbs: 1 g
- Protein: 62 g
- Fiber: 0.2 g

Pork Tenderloin

Preparation time: 10 minutes
Cooking time: 25 minutes
Servings: 4

Ingredients:

- 1.75 pounds Pork tenderloin, fat trimmed
- ½ teaspoon onion powder
- ¼ teaspoon garlic powder
- 1 ½ teaspoon salt
- 1 tablespoon smoked paprika
- ¼ teaspoon cayenne powder
- 1 teaspoon ground mustard
- 2 tablespoons coconut sugar
- ½ teaspoon ground black pepper
- ½ tablespoon olive oil

Method:

1. Switch on the air fryer, insert fryer basket, grease it with non-stick cooking oil spray, then shut with its lid, set the fryer at 400 degrees F, and preheat for 5 minutes.
2. Meanwhile, take a small bowl, place all the spices in it and then stir until combined.
3. Coat the pork with oil, sprinkle the spice mix and then rub well until coated.
4. Open the fryer, arrange pork tenderloin in the air fryer basket, spray oil on the food, close with its lid and cook for 25 minutes until thoroughly cooked, turning halfway.
5. Serve straight away.

Nutrition Value:

- Calories: 335.6 Cal
- Fat: 10.7 g
- Carbs: 14.6 g
- Protein: 42.2 g
- Fiber: 0.1 g

Pork Chops

Preparation time: 10 minutes
Cooking time: 12 minutes
Servings: 2

Ingredients:

- 2 pork chops, center-cut, bone-in, each about 2-inches thick
- ½ teaspoon onion powder
- 1 ½ teaspoons salt
- ¼ teaspoon garlic powder
- 1 tablespoon paprika
- 1 ½ teaspoon ground black pepper
- 2 tablespoons coconut sugar
- 1 teaspoon ground mustard
- 2 tablespoons olive oil

Method:

1. Switch on the air fryer, insert fryer basket, grease it with non-stick cooking oil spray, then shut with its lid, set the fryer at 400 degrees F, and preheat for 5 minutes.
2. Meanwhile, take a small bowl, place all the spices in it and then stir until well mixed.
3. Rub the pork chops with oil and then season with the spice mix until well coated.
4. Open the fryer, arrange the pork chops in the air fryer basket in a single layer, spray oil on the food, close with its lid and cook for 12 minutes until thoroughly cooked, turning halfway.
5. Serve straight away.

Nutrition Value:

- Calories: 300 Cal
- Fat: 14.1 g
- Carbs: 3 g
- Protein: 38.9 g
- Fiber: 1 g

Super Quick Pork Chops

Preparation time: 10 minutes
Cooking time: 12 minutes
Servings: 3

Ingredients:

- 3 pork loin chops, each about 6 ounces
- 1 teaspoon minced garlic
- 1 teaspoon salt
- 1 tablespoon minced rosemary
- 1 teaspoon ground black pepper
- 4 ounces coconut butter, melted

Method:

1. Switch on the air fryer, insert fryer basket, grease it with non-stick cooking oil spray, then shut with its lid, set the fryer at 375 degrees F, and preheat for 5 minutes.
2. Meanwhile, take a small bowl, place garlic in it, add rosemary and butter and then stir until combined.
3. Season the pork chops with salt and black pepper and then drizzle with the rosemary-butter mixture until coated.
4. Open the fryer, arrange the prepared pork chops in the air fryer basket in a single layer, close with its lid and cook for 12 minutes until thoroughly cooked and golden brown, turning halfway.
5. When done, let the pork chops rest for 10 minutes and then serve.

Nutrition Value:

- Calories: 100 Cal
- Fat: 100 g
- Carbs: 100 g
- Protein: 100 g
- Fiber: 100 g

Breaded Pork Chops

Servings: 6
Preparation time: 10 minutes
Cooking time: 24 minutes

Ingredients:

- 6 pork chops, each about 5 ounces, ¾-inch thick, center-cut, boneless
- 1 cup oats
- 1 ½ teaspoon salt
- ½ teaspoon onion powder
- 1/8 teaspoon ground black pepper
- ½ teaspoon garlic powder
- ¼ teaspoon red chili powder
- 1 ¼ teaspoon paprika
- 1 egg
- beaten

Method:

1. Switch on the air fryer, insert fryer basket, grease it with non-stick cooking oil spray, then shut with its lid, set the fryer at 390 degrees F, and preheat for 5 minutes.
2. Meanwhile, prepare the pork chops and for this, season them with ½ teaspoon salt.
3. Take a shallow dish, crack the egg in it and then whisk until blended.
4. Take a separate shallow dish, add oats and remaining ingredients and then stir until combined.
5. Working on one pork chop at a time, dip into the egg and then dredge in oats until coated.
6. Open the fryer, arrange pork chops in the air fryer basket in a single layer, spray oil on the food, close with its lid and cook for 12 minutes until thoroughly cooked and golden brown, turning halfway.
7. Serve straight away.

Nutrition Value:

- Calories: 378 Cal
- Fat: 13 g
- Carbs: 8 g
- Protein: 33 g
- Fiber: 2 g

Pork Bites with Mushrooms

Preparation time: 5 minutes
Cooking time: 18 minutes
Servings: 4

Ingredients:

- 1 pound pork chopped, ¾-inch cubed
- 8 ounces mushrooms, cut in half
- ½ teaspoon garlic powder
- ½ teaspoon salt
- 1 teaspoon soy sauce
- ½ teaspoon ground black pepper
- 2 tablespoons olive oil

Method:

1. Switch on the air fryer, insert fryer basket, grease it with non-stick cooking oil spray, then shut with its lid, set the fryer at 400 degrees F, and preheat for 5 minutes.
2. Meanwhile, take a large bowl, place all the ingredients in it and then toss until combined.
3. Open the fryer, arrange pork and mushroom in the air fryer basket in a single layer, close with its lid and cook for 15 to 18 minutes until thoroughly cooked and golden brown, turning halfway.
4. Serve straight away.

Nutrition Value:

- Calories: 241 Cal
- Fat: 14 g
- Carbs: 2 g
- Protein: 26 g
- Fiber: 1 g

Pork Chops with Brussels Sprouts

Preparation time: 5 minutes
Cooking time: 30 minutes
Servings: 1

Ingredients:

- 1 pork chop, bone-in, center-cut, about 8 ounces
- 6 ounces Brussels sprouts, cut into quarters
- 1/8 teaspoon salt
- 1 teaspoon agave syrup
- ½ teaspoon ground black pepper, divided
- 1 teaspoon mustard paste
- 1 teaspoon olive oil

Method:

1. Switch on the air fryer, insert fryer basket, grease it with non-stick cooking oil spray, then shut with its lid, set the fryer at 400 degrees F, and preheat for 5 minutes.
2. Meanwhile, rub the pork chop with oil and then season with salt and ¼ teaspoon black pepper.
3. Take a medium bowl, place remaining ingredients in it, add Brussels sprouts and then toss until coated.
4. Open the fryer, arrange pork chops and Brussels sprouts in the air fryer basket, close with its lid and cook for 13 minutes until thoroughly cooked and golden brown, turning halfway.
5. Serve straight away.

Nutrition Value:

- Calories: 337 Cal
- Fat: 11 g
- Carbs: 21 g
- Protein: 40 g
- Fiber: 10 g

Meatloaf

Preparation time: 5 minutes
Cooking time: 25 minutes
Servings: 4

Ingredients:

- ½ pound ground beef
- 1 small white onion, peeled, chopped
- ½ pound ground pork
- 2 mushrooms, thickly sliced
- 3 tablespoons oats
- 1 teaspoon salt
- 1 tablespoon chopped thyme
- ½ teaspoon ground black pepper
- 1 egg
- 1 tablespoon olive oil, or more as needed

Method:

1. Switch on the air fryer, insert fryer basket, then shut with its lid, set the fryer at 392 degrees F, and preheat for 5 minutes.
2. Meanwhile, take a large bowl, place all the ingredients in it except for mushroom and oil and then stir until well combined.
3. Take a baking pan that fits into the air fryer basket, spoon the meat mixture in it, press the mushroom slices on top and then drizzle with oil.
4. Open the fryer, place the baking pan in the air fryer basket, close with its lid and cook for 25 minutes until thoroughly cooked and the top turned golden brown.
5. Serve straight away.

Nutrition Value:

- Calories: 297 Cal
- Fat: 18.8 g
- Carbs: 6 g
- Protein: 24.8 g
- Fiber: 0.8 g

Crispy Pork Chops

Preparation time: 10 minutes
Cooking time: 12 minutes
Servings: 6

Ingredients:

- 1 ½ pound pork chops, boneless
- 1/3 cup oats
- 1 teaspoon garlic powder
- 1 teaspoon paprika
- 1 teaspoon creole seasoning
- ¼ cup vegan grated parmesan cheese

Method:

1. Switch on the air fryer, insert fryer basket, grease it with non-stick cooking oil spray, then shut with its lid, set the fryer at 360 degrees F, and preheat for 5 minutes.
2. Meanwhile, take a large plastic bag and place all the ingredients in it.
3. Seal the bag and then turn it upside down until pork chops are coated with the oat mixture.
4. Open the fryer, arrange pork chops in the air fryer basket in a single layer, spray oil on the food, close with its lid and cook for 12 minutes until thoroughly cooked and golden brown, turning halfway.
5. Serve straight away.

Nutrition Value:

- Calories: 231 Cal
- Fat: 12 g
- Carbs: 2 g
- Protein: 27 g
- Fiber: 1 g

Garlic Butter Pork Chops

Preparation time: 10 minutes
Cooking time: 30 minutes
Servings: 2

Ingredients:

- 4 pork chops, each about 6 ounces
- 2 teaspoons minced garlic
- 1 teaspoon salt
- 1 teaspoon ground black pepper
- 2 teaspoons chopped parsley
- 1 tablespoon coconut butter
- 1 tablespoon coconut oil

Method:

1. Take a small bowl, place garlic, butter and coconut oil, add all the seasonings and then stir until mixed.
2. Rub the spice mix on both sides of pork chops, seal them in aluminum foil and then let them marinate for a minimum of 1 hour in the refrigerator.
3. When ready to cook, switch on the air fryer, insert the fryer basket, grease it with non-stick cooking oil spray, then shut with its lid, set the fryer at 350 degrees F, and preheat for 5 minutes.
4. Meanwhile, remove pork chops from the refrigerator and uncover them.
5. Open the fryer, arrange the pork chops in the air fryer basket in a single layer, close with its lid and cook for 15 minutes until thoroughly cooked and golden brown, turning halfway.
6. Serve straight away.

Nutrition Value:

- Calories: 524 Cal
- Fat: 29 g
- Carbs: 2 g
- Protein: 58 g
- Fiber: 1 g

Pulled Pork

Preparation time: 5 minutes
Cooking time: 30 minutes
Servings: 8

Ingredients:

- 4 pounds pork shoulder, boneless
- 2 teaspoons onion powder
- 2 teaspoons garlic powder
- 2 teaspoons salt
- 2 tablespoons red chili powder
- 1 tablespoon parsley
- 2 teaspoons paprika
- 2 teaspoons cumin

Method:

1. Switch on the air fryer, insert fryer basket, grease it with non-stick cooking oil spray, then shut with its lid, set the fryer at 350 degrees F, and preheat for 5 minutes.
2. Meanwhile, take a small bowl, place all the spices in it, stir until combined and then rub this mixture all over the pork shoulder.
3. Open the fryer, arrange pork shoulder in the air fryer basket, spray oil on the food, close with its lid and cook for 90 minutes until tender and golden brown, turning halfway.
4. Serve straight away.

Nutrition Value:

- Calories: 537 Cal
- Fat: 35.5 g
- Carbs: 0.7 g
- Protein: 42.6 g
- Fiber: 0.8 g

Glazed Pork Tenderloin

Preparation time: 10 minutes
Cooking time: 20 minutes
Servings: 4

Ingredients:

- 1.5-pound pork tenderloin, fat trimmed
- 2 cloves of garlic, peeled, sliced
- 1 teaspoon dried rosemary
- ¼ teaspoon salt
- 3 tablespoons coconut sugar
- ⅛ teaspoon ground black pepper
- 1 teaspoon Italian seasoning
- ¼ cup yellow mustard

Method:

1. Prepare the pork tenderloin and for this, make some slits in it and then stuff with garlic.
2. Take a small bowl, place all the seasonings and mustard in it and then stir until combined.
3. Rub the prepared spice mix all over the pork and then let it marinate for a minimum of 2 hours in the refrigerator.
4. When ready to cook, switch on the air fryer, insert the fryer basket, grease it with non-stick cooking oil spray, then shut with its lid, set the fryer at 400 degrees F, and preheat for 5 minutes.
5. Open the fryer, arrange the marinated pork tenderloin in the air fryer basket, spray oil on the food, close with its lid and cook for 20 minutes until thoroughly cooked, turning halfway.
6. When done, let the pork tenderloin rest for 5 minutes, cut it into slices and then serve.

Nutrition Value:

- Calories: 390 Cal
- Fat: 11 g
- Carbs: 11 g
- Protein: 59 g
- Fiber: 1 g

Pork Tenderloin with Broccoli

Preparation time: 10 minutes
Cooking time: 30 minutes
Servings: 4

Ingredients:

For the Pork:

- 1 ½ pound pork tenderloin, fat trimmed
- ¼ teaspoon garlic powder
- 1 teaspoon salt
- 1 teaspoon ground mustard

- ½ teaspoon ground black pepper
- 1 tablespoon smoked paprika
- 2 tablespoons coconut sugar
- ¼ teaspoon cayenne pepper
- 1 tablespoon olive oil

For the Broccoli:

- 4 cups chopped broccoli florets
- 1 tablespoon olive oil

- 1 teaspoon salt
- ½ teaspoon ground black pepper

Method:

1. Switch on the air fryer, insert fryer basket, grease it with non-stick cooking oil spray, then shut with its lid, set the fryer at 400 degrees F, and preheat for 5 minutes.
2. Meanwhile, take a small bowl, place all the spices in it and then stir until combined.
3. Brush oil all over the pork tenderloin, rub with the spice mix and let it rest for 5 minutes.
4. Open the fryer, arrange pork tenderloin in the air fryer basket in a single layer, spray oil on the food, close with its lid and cook for 20 minutes until thoroughly cooked, turning halfway.
5. Meanwhile, take a heat-proof bowl, place broccoli florets in it, drizzle with 1 tablespoon water and then microwave at high heat setting for 3 minutes until tender.
6. Drain the broccoli florets, season with salt and black pepper, drizzle with oil and then toss until coated.
7. When the pork tenderloin has cooked, let it rest on the cutting board for 5 minutes and then cut into slices.
8. While the pork tenderloin is resting
9. transfer broccoli florets into the air fryer basket and cook for 10 minutes, tossing halfway.
10. Serve the pork tenderloin with broccoli florets.

Nutrition Value:

- Calories: 271 Cal
- Fat: 11.1 g
- Carbs: 14 g

- Protein: 29.5 g
- Fiber: 2.8 g

Southern Style Pork Chops

Preparation time: 10 minutes
Cooking time: 15 minutes
Servings: 4

Ingredients:

- 4 pork chops, boneless
- ½ teaspoon salt
- ¼ cup almond flour
- ½ teaspoon ground black pepper
- 3 tablespoons buttermilk

Method:

1. Prepare the pork chops and for this, season them with salt and black pepper and then drizzle with milk.
2. Take a large plastic bag
3. place flour in it and then add seasoned pork chops.
4. Seal the bag
5. turn it upside down until pork chops are coated in flour and then let them marinate for 30 minutes.
6. When ready to cook, switch on the air fryer, insert the fryer basket, grease it with non-stick cooking oil spray, then shut with its lid, set the fryer at 380 degrees F, and preheat for 5 minutes.
7. Open the fryer, arrange the pork chops in the air fryer basket in a single layer, spray oil on the food, close with its lid and cook for 15 minutes until thoroughly cooked and golden brown, turning halfway.
8. Serve straight away.

Nutrition Value:

- Calories: 296 Cal
- Fat: 13.4 g
- Carbs: 23.4 g
- Protein: 20 g
- Fiber: 0.3 g

Chapter 6: Lean & Green Seafood

Simple Tilapia

Preparation time: 10 minutes
Cooking time: 20 minutes
Servings: 4

Ingredients:

- 4 fillets of tilapia, each about 6 ounces
- 2 cups oats
- 1 teaspoon garlic powder
- 1 tablespoon salt
- 2 tablespoons paprika
- 2 tablespoons lemon pepper seasoning
- 1 egg
- 1 teaspoon water, warm

Method:

1. Switch on the air fryer, insert fryer basket, grease it with non-stick cooking oil spray, then shut with its lid, set the fryer at 350 degrees F, and preheat for 5 minutes.
2. Meanwhile, crack the egg in a shallow dish, add water and then whisk until blended.
3. Take a separate shallow dish, place oats in it, add remaining ingredients except for fillets and then stir until mixed.
4. Working on one fillet at a time, dip into the egg and then dredge in the oat mixture until coated.
5. Open the fryer, arrange fillets in the air fryer basket in a single layer, spray oil on the food, close with its lid and cook for 20 minutes until thoroughly cooked and golden brown, turning halfway.
6. Serve straight away.

Nutrition Value:

- Calories: 350 Cal
- Fat: 15 g
- Carbs: 43 g
- Protein: 76 g
- Fiber: 5 g

Blackened Fish Lettuce Wrap

Preparation time: 5 minutes
Cooking time: 10 minutes
Servings: 4

Ingredients:

- 1 pound Mahi-Mahi fillets
- 2 ½ tablespoon Cajun seasoning
- 2 tablespoons olive oil

For Serving:

- 4 large lettuce leaves
- ½ cup mango salsa
- ½ cup shredded cabbage

Method:

1. Switch on the air fryer, insert fryer basket, grease it with non-stick cooking oil spray, then shut with its lid, set the fryer at 360 degrees F, and preheat for 5 minutes.
2. Meanwhile, prepare the fish and for this, brush the fillets with oil and then season with the Cajun seasoning until coated.
3. Open the fryer, arrange fillets in the air fryer basket, spray oil on the food, close with its lid and cook for 10 minutes until thoroughly cooked and golden brown, turning halfway.
4. When done, evenly divide Mahi-Mahi fillets among the lettuce leaves, top with mango salsa and cabbage and then serve.

Nutrition Value:

- Calories: 247 Cal
- Fat: 3 g
- Carbs: 32 g
- Protein: 25 g
- Fiber: 5 g

Cajun Salmon

Preparation time: 10 minutes
Cooking time: 10 minutes
Servings: 1

Ingredients:

- 1 fillet of salmon, about 7 ounces
- 1 teaspoon Cajun seasoning
- 2 tablespoons lemon juice

Method:

1. Switch on the air fryer, insert fryer basket, grease it with non-stick cooking oil spray, then shut with its lid, set the fryer at 350 degrees F, and preheat for 5 minutes.
2. Meanwhile, prepare the salmon and for this, season it with Cajun seasoning
3. Open the fryer, arrange salmon in the air fryer basket, spray oil on the food, close with its lid and cook for 8 to 10 minutes until thoroughly cooked, turning halfway.
4. Serve straight away.

Nutrition Value:

- Calories: 231 Cal
- Fat: 14 g
- Carbs: 2 g
- Protein: 22 g
- Fiber: 0.5 g

Garlic and Lemon Fish

Preparation time: 10 minutes
Cooking time: 15 minutes
Servings: 2

Ingredients:

- 2 fillets of tilapia, each about 6 ounces
- ½ teaspoon onion powder
- 1 teaspoon salt
- ½ teaspoon garlic powder
- ½ teaspoon ground black pepper
- ½ teaspoon lemon pepper seasoning
- 2 tablespoons olive oil
- 2 tablespoons chopped parsley

Method:

1. Switch on the air fryer, insert fryer basket, line it with perforated parchment paper, grease it with non-stick cooking oil spray, then shut with its lid, set the fryer at 360 degrees F, and preheat for 5 minutes.
2. Meanwhile, brush the fillets with oil and then season with salt, black pepper, onion powder, garlic powder and lemon pepper seasoning until coated.
3. Open the fryer, arrange tilapia in the air fryer basket in a single layer, close with its lid and cook for 12 to 15 minutes until thoroughly cooked and golden brown, turning halfway.
4. When done, sprinkle parsley over the tilapia fillets and then serve straight away.

Nutrition Value:

- Calories: 169 Cal
- Fat: 3 g
- Carbs: 1 g
- Protein: 34 g
- Fiber: 1 g

Lemon and Garlic Salmon

Preparation time: 5 minutes
Cooking time: 14 minutes
Servings: 4

Ingredients:

- 4 fillets of salmon, each about 6 ounces
- 1 lemon, cut into slices
- 1 teaspoon sea salt
- 2 teaspoons garlic powder
- 2 teaspoons Italian seasoning
- 1 teaspoon ground black pepper
- 2 tablespoons olive oil
- 1 teaspoon lemon juice

Method:

1. Switch on the air fryer, insert fryer basket, grease it with non-stick cooking oil spray, then shut with its lid, set the fryer at 400 degrees F, and preheat for 5 minutes.
2. Meanwhile, prepare the salmon and for this, rub with oil and lemon juice and then season with salt, black pepper and Italian seasoning
3. Open the fryer, arrange salmon in the air fryer basket, scatter lemon slices on top, spray oil on the food, close with its lid and cook for 14 minutes until thoroughly cooked.
4. Serve straight away.

Nutrition Value:

- Calories: 462 Cal
- Fat: 28 g
- Carbs: 13 g
- Protein: 39 g
- Fiber: 2 g

Salmon Cakes

Preparation time: 5 minutes
Cooking time: 30 minutes
Servings: 2

Ingredients:

- 15 ounces canned salmon, without bones and skin
- 1 teaspoon salt
- ½ cup oats
- ¼ teaspoon ground black pepper
- 2 tablespoons chopped dill
- 2 teaspoons mustard paste
- 1 egg
- 2 tablespoons vegan mayonnaise

Method:

1. Switch on the air fryer, insert fryer basket, grease it with non-stick cooking oil spray, then shut with its lid, set the fryer at 390 degrees F, and preheat for 5 minutes.
2. Meanwhile, take a large bowl, place salmon in it, add remaining ingredients and then shape the mixture into four evenly sized patties.
3. Open the fryer, arrange salmon patties in the air fryer basket in a single layer, spray oil on the food, close with its lid and cook for 12 minutes until thoroughly cooked and golden brown, turning halfway.
4. Serve straight away.

Nutrition Value:

- Calories: 517 Cal
- Fat: 26.7 g
- Carbs: 14.7 g
- Protein: 51.8 g
- Fiber: 2.1 g

Lemon Pepper Shrimp

Preparation time: 5 minutes
Cooking time: 8 minutes
Servings: 2

Ingredients:

- 12 ounces shrimp, peeled, deveined
- ¼ teaspoon garlic powder
- 1 teaspoon lemon pepper
- 1 lemon, juiced
- ¼ teaspoon paprika
- 1 tablespoon olive oil

Method:

1. Switch on the air fryer, insert fryer basket, grease it with non-stick cooking oil spray, then shut with its lid, set the fryer at 400 degrees F, and preheat for 5 minutes.
2. Meanwhile, take a large bowl, place all the ingredients in it and then stir until well combined.
3. Open the fryer, arrange shrimps in the air fryer basket in a single layer, close with its lid and cook for 6 to 8 minutes until thoroughly cooked, turning halfway.
4. Serve straight away.

Nutrition Value:

- Calories: 215 Cal
- Fat: 8.6 g
- Carbs: 12.6 g
- Protein: 28.6 g
- Fiber: 5.5 g

Fish Nuggets

Preparation time: 10 minutes
Cooking time: 10 minutes
Servings: 4

Ingredients:

- 1 ½ pound cod fillets, cut into cubes
- ½ cup oats
- ½ cup coconut flour
- 1/3 teaspoon salt
- 1 teaspoon lemon and pepper seasoning
- ¼ teaspoon ground black pepper
- ¼ teaspoon dried thyme
- 3 tablespoons water
- 2 eggs

Method:

1. Switch on the air fryer, insert fryer basket, grease it with non-stick cooking oil spray, then shut with its lid, set the fryer at 400 degrees F, and preheat for 5 minutes.
2. Meanwhile, take a shallow dish and place coconut in it.
3. Take a medium bowl, crack the eggs in it, add water and then whisk until blended.
4. Take a separate shallow dish, place oats in it, add salt, lemon and pepper seasoning
5. black pepper and thyme and then stir until mixed.
6. Working on one fish cube at a time, dredge in flour, dip into the egg and then dredge in oats mixture until coated.
7. Open the fryer, arrange nuggets in the air fryer basket in a single layer, spray oil on the food, close with its lid and cook for 10 minutes until thoroughly cooked and golden brown, turning halfway.
8. Serve straight away.

Nutrition Value:

- Calories: 328 Cal
- Fat: 11 g
- Carbs: 7 g
- Protein: 43.4 g
- Fiber: 2.8 g

Cauliflower Rice with Shrimps

Preparation time: 10 minutes
Cooking time: 25 minutes
Servings: 2

Ingredients:

- ½ pound shrimps, peeled, deveined
- ¼ teaspoon salt

For the Rice:

- 24 ounces cauliflower rice
- ¼ cup chopped green onions
- 1 ½ tablespoon sesame oil

For the Eggs:

- 1 egg
- 1/8 teaspoon salt

- 1/8 teaspoon ground black pepper

- ½ tablespoon soy sauce
- ¼ teaspoon salt
- ½ teaspoon ground black pepper

- 1/8 teaspoon ground black pepper

Method:

1. Switch on the air fryer, insert fryer basket, line it with parchment sheet, grease it with non-stick cooking oil spray, then shut with its lid, set the fryer at 350 degrees F, and preheat for 5 minutes.
2. Meanwhile, take a large bowl, place shrimps in it, add salt and black pepper and then toss until coated.
3. Meanwhile, take a heatproof bowl, place cauliflower rice in it and then microwave for 5 minutes.
4. Drain the cauliflower rice, add remaining ingredients for the rice and then stir until mixed.
5. Spoon the prepared cauliflower rice into the fryer basket, close with its lid and cook for 15 minutes until thoroughly cooked, stirring halfway.
6. Then top the rice with shrimps and continue cooking for 5 minutes.
7. Meanwhile, crack the egg in a bowl, add salt and black pepper and then whisk until blended.
8. Pour the egg mixture into the cauliflower rice and shrimps mixture, toss until mixed and then continue cooking for 5 minutes.
9. Serve straight away.

Nutrition Value:

- Calories: 344 Cal
- Fat: 15 g
- Carbs: 29 g

- Protein: 23 g
- Fiber: 2 g

Fish Skewers

Preparation time: 35 minutes
Cooking time: 8 minutes
Servings: 4

Ingredients:

- 2 fillets of salmon, 1-inch cubed
- 1 medium red bell pepper, cored, cubed
- 1 medium orange bell pepper, cored, cubed
- 1 medium green bell pepper, cored, cubed

For the Marinade:

- 2 teaspoons minced garlic
- 1 teaspoon salt
- 2 teaspoons dried thyme
- ½ teaspoon ground black pepper
- 2 teaspoons dried oregano
- 1 teaspoon ground cumin
- ½ cup olive oil
- ½ teaspoon ground coriander
- 2 tablespoons lemon juice

Method:

1. Take a small bowl, place all the ingredients for the marinade in it and then stir until combined.
2. Take a large plastic bag
3. pour the marinade mixture in it, and then add salmon pieces and vegetable pieces in it.
4. Seal the bag
5. turn it upside down until salmon and vegetable pieces are coated in marinate and then marinate in the refrigerator for a minimum of 30 minutes.
6. When ready to cook, switch on the air fryer, insert the fryer basket, grease it with non-stick cooking oil spray, then shut with its lid, set the fryer at 350 degrees F, and preheat for 5 minutes.
7. Meanwhile, thread salmon pieces and vegetable pieces into the wooden skewers.
8. Open the fryer, arrange skewers in the air fryer basket in a single layer, spray oil on the food, close with its lid and cook for 6 to 8 minutes until thoroughly cooked, turning halfway.
9. Serve straight away.

Nutrition Value:

- Calories: 255.4 Cal
- Fat: 6.2 g
- Carbs: 12 g
- Protein: 30.2 g
- Fiber: 2.8 g

Tuna Patties

Preparation time: 5 minutes
Cooking time: 10 minutes
Servings: 10

Ingredients:

- 15 ounces canned tuna, drained
- 1 stalk of celery, chopped
- ½ cup oats
- 3 tablespoons minced white onion
- ½ teaspoon garlic powder
- ¼ teaspoon salt
- ¼ teaspoon dried basil
- 1/8 teaspoon ground black pepper
- ¼ teaspoon dried thyme
- 1 medium lemon, zested
- 2 eggs
- 1 tablespoon lemon juice
- 3 tablespoons vegan grated parmesan cheese

Method:

1. Switch on the air fryer, insert fryer basket, grease it with non-stick cooking oil spray, then shut with its lid, set the fryer at 360 degrees F, and preheat for 5 minutes.
2. Meanwhile, take a large bowl, place all the ingredients in it, stir until well combined and then shape the mixture evenly into ten patties.
3. Open the fryer, arrange tuna patties in the air fryer basket in a single layer, spray oil on the food, close with its lid and cook for 10 minutes until thoroughly cooked and golden brown, turning halfway.
4. Serve straight away.

Nutrition Value:

- Calories: 101 Cal
- Fat: 3 g
- Carbs: 5 g
- Protein: 13 g
- Fiber: 1 g

Fish Sticks

Preparation time: 10 minutes
Cooking time: 12 minutes
Servings: 4

Ingredients:

- 1 pound cod fillets, skinless, cut into 1-inch strips
- 1/2 teaspoon salt
- ¾ cup oats
- 1/2 teaspoon paprika
- ½ teaspoon lemon and pepper seasoning
- 1 egg

Method:

1. Switch on the air fryer, insert fryer basket, grease it with non-stick cooking oil spray, then shut with its lid, set the fryer at 400 degrees F, and preheat for 5 minutes.
2. Meanwhile, take a shallow dish, crack the egg in it and then whisk until blended.
3. Take a separate shallow dish, place oats in it, add salt, paprika and lemon and pepper seasoning and then stir until mixed.
4. Working on one fish stick at a time, dip into the egg and then dredge in oats mixture until coated.
5. Open the fryer, arrange fish sticks in the air fryer basket in a single layer, spray oil on the food, close with its lid and cook for 12 minutes until thoroughly cooked, turning halfway.
6. Serve straight away.

Nutrition Value:

- Calories: 200 Cal
- Fat: 3 g
- Carbs: 15 g
- Protein: 18 g
- Fiber: 3 g

Lemon, Pepper and Paprika Salmon

Preparation time: 5 minutes
Cooking time: 10 minutes
Servings: 2

Ingredients:

- 2 fillets of salmon, each about 1 ½ inch thick
- 1 teaspoon salt
- 1 teaspoon paprika
- 1 teaspoon ground black pepper
- ½ of lemon, juiced
- 1 tablespoon olive oil
- 1 lemon, cut into slices

Method:

1. Switch on the air fryer, insert fryer basket, grease it with non-stick cooking oil spray, then shut with its lid, set the fryer at 390 degrees F, and preheat for 5 minutes.
2. Meanwhile, rub salmon with oil and lemon juice and then season with salt, black pepper and paprika until coated.
3. Open the fryer, arrange salmon fillets in the air fryer basket in a single layer, spray oil on the food, close with its lid and cook for 10 minutes until thoroughly cooked, turning halfway.
4. Serve straight away.

Nutrition Value:

- Calories: 234 Cal
- Fat: 14 g
- Carbs: 2 g
- Protein: 25 g
- Fiber: 0 g

Pecan Crusted Halibut

Preparation time: 10 minutes
Cooking time: 8 minutes
Servings: 4

Ingredients:

- 4 fillets of halibut, skinless, each about 4 ounces
- ½ cup pecans, ground
- ½ cup corn starch
- ½ cup oats
- 3 tablespoons lemon pepper seasoning
- 2 egg whites
- ½ cup white wine

Method:

1. Switch on the air fryer, insert fryer basket, grease it with non-stick cooking oil spray, then shut with its lid, set the fryer at 375 degrees F, and preheat for 5 minutes.
2. Meanwhile, take a medium bowl, place the egg whites in it, and then whisk in cornstarch until blended.
3. Whisk in wine until well combined, and then whisk in 1 ½ tablespoon lemon pepper seasoning until smooth batter comes together.
4. Take a shallow dish and then place oats in it.
5. Working on one halibut fillet at a time, season it with salt and lemon pepper, dip into the prepared egg whites mixture and then dredge in pecan until coated.
6. Open the fryer, arrange halibut fillets in the air fryer basket in a single layer, spray oil on the food, close with its lid and cook for 10 minutes until thoroughly cooked and golden brown, turning halfway.
7. Serve straight away.

Nutrition Value:

- Calories: 432 Cal
- Fat: 16 g
- Carbs: 31 g
- Protein: 37 g
- Fiber: 3 g

Salmon and Asparagus

Preparation time: 10 minutes
Cooking time: 10 minutes
Servings: 4

Ingredients:

- 1 bunch of asparagus
- 2 tablespoons chopped parsley
- 2 fillets of salmon, deboned, each about 6 ounces
- 2 tablespoons chopped dill
- 1 ½ teaspoon salt
- 1 ½ tablespoon lemon juice
- ¾ teaspoon ground black pepper
- 1 tablespoon olive oil

Method:

1. Switch on the air fryer, insert fryer basket, grease it with non-stick cooking oil spray, then shut with its lid, set the fryer at 400 degrees F, and preheat for 5 minutes.
2. Meanwhile, take a small bowl, pour in olive oil and lemon juice, add parsley, dill and half of salt and black pepper and then stir until combined.
3. Prepare the salmon and for this, rub it with three-fourth of the parsley-dill mixture and then add the remaining mixture into a large bowl.
4. Add asparagus to the bowl containing the remaining parsley-dill mixture and then toss until coated.
5. Open the fryer, arrange asparagus in the air fryer basket in an even layer, top with salmon, close with its lid, and cook for 8 to 10 minutes until thoroughly cooked, turning salmon halfway.
6. Serve straight away.

Nutrition Value:

- Calories: 391 Cal
- Fat: 19 g
- Carbs: 9 g
- Protein: 48 g
- Fiber: 5 g

Blackened Tilapia Fillets

Preparation time: 5 minutes
Cooking time: 15 minutes
Servings: 4

Ingredients:

- 2 fillets of tilapia, each about 4 ounces
- 1 tablespoon olive oil

For the Seasoning:

- 1 ½ teaspoon onion powder
- ¼ teaspoon garlic powder
- ½ teaspoon sea salt
- ½ teaspoon ground thyme
- ½ teaspoon cayenne pepper
- ½ teaspoon ground black pepper
- ½ teaspoon dried oregano
- 1 ½ tablespoon smoked paprika

Method:

1. Switch on the air fryer, insert fryer basket, grease it with non-stick cooking oil spray, then shut with its lid, set the fryer at 350 degrees F, and preheat for 5 minutes.
2. Meanwhile, take a shallow dish, place all the ingredients for the seasoning in it and then stir until combined.
3. Rub the tilapia fillets with oil and then dredge in the seasoning mixture until coated.
4. Open the fryer, arrange tilapia fillets in the air fryer basket in a single layer, spray oil on the food, close with its lid and cook for 12 to 15 minutes until thoroughly cooked, turning halfway.
5. Serve straight away.

Nutrition Value:

- Calories: 178 Cal
- Fat: 10 g
- Carbs: 5 g
- Protein: 21 g
- Fiber: 1 g

Crispy Ranch Fish

Preparation time: 10 minutes
Cooking time: 10 minutes
Servings: 6

Ingredients:

- 6 fillets of tilapia, each about 6 ounces
- 2 cups oats
- 3 tablespoon ranch seasoning
- 1 teaspoon garlic powder
- ½ teaspoon salt
- ¼ teaspoon ground black pepper
- 2 eggs

Method:

1. Switch on the air fryer, insert fryer basket, grease it with non-stick cooking oil spray, then shut with its lid, set the fryer at 400 degrees F, and preheat for 5 minutes.
2. Meanwhile, take a shallow dish, place oats in it, add salt, black pepper and ranch seasoning in it and then stir until combined.
3. Take a separate shallow dish, crack the eggs in it and then whisk until blended.
4. Working on one fillet at a time, dip into the egg and then dredge in oats mixture until well coated.
5. Open the fryer, arrange tilapia in the air fryer basket in a single layer, spray oil on the food, close with its lid and cook for 10 minutes until thoroughly cooked and golden brown, turning halfway.
6. Serve straight away.

Nutrition Value:

- Calories: 310 Cal
- Fat: 13.3 g
- Carbs: 18.9 g
- Protein: 26.5 g
- Fiber: 1.1 g

Crab Cakes

Preparation time: 5 minutes
Cooking time: 10 minutes
Servings: 4

Ingredients:

- ¼ cup chopped red bell pepper
- 8 ounces crab meat
- 2 green onions, chopped
- 2 tablespoons oats
- 1 tablespoon Dijon mustard
- 1 teaspoon Old bay seasoning
- 2 tablespoons vegan mayonnaise

Method:

1. Switch on the air fryer, insert fryer basket, line it with perforated baking paper, grease it with non-stick cooking oil spray, then shut with its lid, set the fryer at 370 degrees F, and preheat for 5 minutes.
2. Meanwhile, take a large bowl, place crab meat in it, add remaining ingredients in it, stir until combined and then shape the mixture into four evenly sized patties.
3. Open the fryer, arrange food in the air fryer basket in a single layer, spray oil on the food, close with its lid and cook for 10 minutes until thoroughly cooked, turning halfway.
4. Serve straight away.

Nutrition Value:

- Calories: 123 Cal
- Fat: 6 g
- Carbs: 5 g
- Protein: 12 g
- Fiber: 1 g

Fish Cakes with Cilantro

Preparation time: 5 minutes
Cooking time: 10 minutes
Servings: 2

Ingredients:

- 2/3 cup oats
- 10 ounces chopped catfish
- ¼ teaspoon salt
- 2 tablespoons sweet chili sauce
- ¼ teaspoon ground black pepper
- 2 tablespoons vegan mayonnaise
- 3 tablespoons chopped cilantro
- 1 egg

Method:

1. Switch on the air fryer, insert fryer basket, grease it with non-stick cooking oil spray, then shut with its lid, set the fryer at 400 degrees F, and preheat for 5 minutes.
2. Meanwhile, take a large bowl, place all the ingredients in it, stir until combined and then shape the mixture into four evenly sized patties.
3. Open the fryer, arrange fish cakes in the air fryer basket in a single layer, spray oil on the food, close with its lid and cook for 10 minutes until thoroughly cooked and golden brown, turning halfway.
4. Serve straight away.

Nutrition Value:

- Calories: 399 Cal
- Fat: 15.5 g
- Carbs: 27.9 g
- Protein: 34.6 g
- Fiber: 2.8 g

Cod

Preparation time: 5 minutes
Cooking time: 16 minutes
Servings: 6

Ingredients:

- 1 ½ pound cod, skinless, about 6 pieces
- ½ teaspoon salt
- ½ teaspoon garlic powder
- 1 teaspoon smoked paprika
- 1/8 teaspoon ground black pepper
- 2 teaspoon old bay seasoning
- ½ cup oats

Method:

1. Switch on the air fryer, insert fryer basket, grease it with non-stick cooking oil spray, then shut with its lid, set the fryer at 390 degrees F, and preheat for 5 minutes.
2. Meanwhile, take a shallow dish, place all the ingredients except for the cod pieces and then stir until mixed.
3. Working on one fish piece at a time, dredge it in oats mixture until coated.
4. Open the fryer, arrange the cod pieces in the air fryer basket in a single layer, spray oil on the food, close with its lid and cook for 16 minutes until thoroughly cooked, turning halfway.
5. Serve straight away.

Nutrition Value:

- Calories: 70 Cal
- Fat: 1 g
- Carbs: 15 g
- Protein: 2 g
- Fiber: 1 g

Chapter 7: Green & Side Dishes

Quiche

Preparation time: 5 minutes
Cooking time: 10 minutes
Servings: 1

Ingredients:

- 4 florets of broccoli
- 1 tablespoon vegan cheddar cheese
- 4 tablespoons vegan heavy cream
- 1 egg

Method:

1. Switch on the air fryer, insert fryer basket, then shut with its lid, set the fryer at 325 degrees F, and preheat for 5 minutes.
2. Meanwhile, take a 5-inch heat-proof quiche dish, grease it with oil, crack the egg in it and then whisk in cream.
3. Scatter broccoli florets on top of the mixture and then sprinkle with cheese.
4. Open the fryer, place the quiche dish in the air fryer basket, close with its lid and cook for 10 minutes until thoroughly cooked, turning halfway.
5. Serve straight away.

Nutrition Value:

- Calories: 656 Cal
- Fat: 58 g
- Carbs: 18 g
- Protein: 21 g
- Fiber: 6 g

Artichoke Hearts

Preparation time: 5 minutes
Cooking time: 8 minutes
Servings: 4

Ingredients:

- 14 ounces canned artichoke hearts, quarter, drained
- 1/8 teaspoon garlic powder
- ¼ teaspoon salt
- 1/8 teaspoon ground black pepper
- ¼ teaspoon Italian seasoning
- 2 teaspoons vegan grated parmesan cheese
- 1 tablespoon olive oil

Method:

1. Switch on the air fryer, insert fryer basket, grease it with non-stick cooking oil spray, then shut with its lid, set the fryer at 390 degrees F, and preheat for 5 minutes.
2. Meanwhile, pat dry the artichoke hearts, place them in a large bowl, add remaining ingredients and then toss until coated.
3. Open the fryer, arrange artichoke hearts in the air fryer basket in a single layer, close with its lid and cook for 8 minutes until thoroughly cooked and golden brown, turning halfway.
4. Serve straight away.

Nutrition Value:

- Calories: 67 Cal
- Fat: 3.7 g
- Carbs: 6.6 g
- Protein: 2.6 g
- Fiber: 2.2 g

Cabbage Fritters

Preparation time: 10 minutes
Cooking time: 15 minutes
Servings: 4

Ingredients:

- 1 cup of chopped cabbage
- 1 medium white onion, peeled, chopped
- 1 teaspoon chopped green chili
- 1 teaspoon salt
- 1 teaspoon minced garlic
- 1 teaspoon red chili powder
- ½ teaspoon grated ginger
- 1 teaspoon cumin seeds
- 1 teaspoon ground cumin
- 1 tablespoon chopped coriander leaves

Method:

1. Switch on the air fryer, insert fryer basket, grease it with non-stick cooking oil spray, then shut with its lid, set the fryer at 350 degrees F, and preheat for 5 minutes.
2. Meanwhile, take a large bowl, place all the ingredients in it and then stir until well combined.
3. Open the fryer, spoon the zucchini mixture in the air fryer basket in a single layer, spray oil on the food, close with its lid and cook for 15 minutes until thoroughly cooked and golden brown, turning halfway.
4. Serve straight away.

Nutrition Value:

- Calories: 98.1 Cal
- Fat: 2 g
- Carbs: 10.5 g
- Protein: 2.6 g
- Fiber: 4 g

Kale Deviled Eggs

Preparation time: 10 minutes
Cooking time: 15 minutes
Servings: 6

Ingredients:

- 6 eggs
- 3 tablespoons chopped kale
- 1/8 teaspoon salt
- ½ teaspoon Worcestershire sauce
- 1 teaspoon pickle juice
- 1/8 teaspoon ground black pepper
- ¼ teaspoon hot sauce
- 1 teaspoon Dijon mustard
- 2 tablespoons vegan mayonnaise
- 2 tablespoons vegan coconut yogurt

Method:

1. Switch on the air fryer, insert fryer basket, then shut with its lid, set the fryer at 300 degrees F, and preheat for 5 minutes.
2. Open the fryer, arrange eggs in the air fryer basket in a single layer, close with its lid and cook for 15 minutes until hard-boiled, turning halfway.
3. Take a large bowl filled with chilled water, transfer boiled eggs in it and let them rest for 5 minutes.
4. Drain the eggs, peel the eggs, cut each egg in half and then transfer the egg yolk to a medium bowl.
5. Add remaining ingredients in it, stir until combined and then stuff the mixture into egg whites.
6. Serve straight away.

Nutrition Value:

- Calories: 77 Cal
- Fat: 5 g
- Carbs: 0.6 g
- Protein: 6.3 g
- Fiber: 0 g

Zucchini Strips

Preparation time: 5 minutes
Cooking time: 14 minutes
Servings: 2

Ingredients:

- 2 large zucchini, ½-inch thick sliced lengthwise
- ½ teaspoon garlic powder
- 1/3 teaspoon salt
- ¼ teaspoon ground black pepper
- 2 tablespoons olive oil

Method:

1. Switch on the air fryer, insert fryer basket, grease it with non-stick cooking oil spray, then shut with its lid, set the fryer at 390 degrees F, and preheat for 5 minutes.
2. Meanwhile, brush the zucchini slices with oil and then season with garlic powder, salt and black pepper.
3. Open the fryer, arrange zucchini slices in the air fryer basket in a single layer, close with its lid and cook for 8 to 14 minutes until thoroughly cooked and golden brown, turning halfway.
4. Serve straight away.

Nutrition Value:

- Calories: 36 Cal
- Fat: 1 g
- Carbs: 7 g
- Protein: 2 g
- Fiber: 2 g

Spicy Okra

Preparation time: 10 minutes
Cooking time: 10 minutes
Servings: 6

Ingredients:

- 1 ¼ pound okra, fresh

For the Breading:

- 1 cup oats
- ½ teaspoon garlic powder
- ½ teaspoon salt
- 1 teaspoon paprika
- 1 teaspoon ground coriander
- ¼ teaspoon ground black pepper
- ½ teaspoon red chili powder
- 2 tablespoons chopped parsley

For the Egg Wash:

- ½ teaspoon ground coriander
- 1/8 teaspoon salt
- ½ teaspoon red chili powder
- ½ teaspoon paprika
- 1 egg

Method:

1. Switch on the air fryer, insert fryer basket, grease it with non-stick cooking oil spray, then shut with its lid, set the fryer at 400 degrees F, and preheat for 5 minutes.
2. Meanwhile, prepare the egg wash and for this, crack the egg in a medium bowl, add the remaining ingredients for the egg wash and then whisk until blended.
3. Prepare the breading and for this, take a shallow dish, place all of its ingredients in it and then stir until combined.
4. Working on one okra at a time, dip into the egg wash mixture and then dredge in the breading until coated.
5. Open the fryer, arrange okra in the air fryer basket in a single layer, spray oil on the food, close with its lid and cook for 8 to 10 minutes until thoroughly cooked and golden brown, turning halfway.
6. Serve straight away.

Nutrition Value:

- Calories: 150 Cal
- Fat: 3 g
- Carbs: 23 g
- Protein: 8 g
- Fiber: 4 g

Cauliflower Fritters

Preparation time: 10 minutes
Cooking time: 25 minutes
Servings: 4

Ingredients:

- ¼ of large cauliflower florets, chopped
- ½ cup coconut flour
- 1 ½ tablespoon chopped mint
- ½ cup buttermilk
- 3.5 ounces crumbled feta cheese
- 1 egg
- 3 tablespoons olive oil

Method:

1. Switch on the air fryer, insert fryer basket, grease it with non-stick cooking oil spray, then shut with its lid, set the fryer at 400 degrees F, and preheat for 5 minutes.
2. Meanwhile, take a large bowl, place cauliflower florets, add salt, black pepper and 1 ½ tablespoon and then toss until coated.
3. Open the fryer, place the cauliflower florets in the air fryer basket, close with its lid and cook for 15 minutes until thoroughly cooked, turning halfway.
4. Take a large bowl, crack the egg in it, whisk in flour and then whisk in milk until thick batter comes together.
5. Add cheese and mint, add cooked cauliflower and remaining oil and then stir until well combined.
6. Spoon the cauliflower mixture in the air fryer basket in a single layer, close with its lid and cook for 10 minutes until thoroughly cooked and golden brown, turning halfway.
7. Serve straight away.

Nutrition Value:

- Calories: 263 Cal
- Fat: 18 g
- Carbs: 17 g
- Protein: 9 g
- Fiber: 2 g

Buttermilk Fried Mushrooms

Preparation time: 20 minutes
Cooking time: 12 minutes
Servings: 2

Ingredients:

- 2 cups oyster mushrooms
- 1 teaspoon onion powder
- 1 teaspoon garlic powder
- 1 teaspoon salt
- 1 ½ cup coconut flour
- 1 teaspoon ground black pepper
- 1 teaspoon paprika
- 1 teaspoon ground cumin
- 1 cup buttermilk

Method:

1. Take a large bowl, place mushrooms in it, add milk, toss until coated and then let them marinate for 15 minutes.
2. When ready to cook, switch on the air fryer, insert fryer basket, grease it with non-stick cooking oil spray, then shut with its lid, set the fryer at 375 degrees F, and preheat for 5 minutes.
3. Meanwhile, take a large bowl, place flour in it, add all the spices and then stir until mixed.
4. Working on one mushroom at a time, remove it from buttermilk, dredge into the flour mixture, dip into the buttermilk and then dredge again into the flour mixture until coated.
5. Open the fryer, arrange mushrooms in the air fryer basket in a single layer, spray oil on the food, close with its lid and cook for 12 minutes until thoroughly cooked, turning halfway.
6. Serve straight away.

Nutrition Value:

- Calories: 355 Cal
- Fat: 9.7 g
- Carbs: 57 g
- Protein: 12.4 g
- Fiber: 3 g

Seasoned Rutabaga Fries

Preparation time: 5 minutes
Cooking time: 15 minutes
Servings: 4

Ingredients:

- 1 rutabaga, peeled, cut into 1/2-inch wedges
- ¼ teaspoon garlic powder
- ½ teaspoon onion powder
- ½ teaspoon salt
- 1 teaspoon paprika
- ¼ teaspoon ground black pepper
- ½ teaspoon dried parsley
- 1 tablespoon olive oil

Method:

1. Switch on the air fryer, insert fryer basket, grease it with non-stick cooking oil spray, then shut with its lid, set the fryer at 400 degrees F, and preheat for 5 minutes.
2. Meanwhile, take a large bowl, place rutabaga wedges in it, add remaining ingredients and then toss until coated.
3. Open the fryer, arrange rutabaga wedges in the air fryer basket in a single layer, close with its lid and cook for 15 minutes until thoroughly cooked and golden brown, turning halfway.
4. Serve straight away.

Nutrition Value:

- Calories: 70 Cal
- Fat: 4 g
- Carbs: 9 g
- Protein: 1 g
- Fiber: 2 g

Zucchini Fritters

Preparation time: 15 minutes
Cooking time: 12 minutes
Servings: 4

Ingredients:

- 2 large zucchini, grated
- ¼ teaspoon onion powder
- 3 tablespoons coconut flour
- 1 teaspoon garlic powder
- 1 tablespoon salt
- ¼ teaspoon ground black pepper
- ¼ teaspoon paprika
- 1 egg

Method:

1. Take a large bowl, place grated zucchini in it, stir in salt and then let it rest for 10 minutes.
2. Drain the zucchini, wrap it in a cheesecloth and then twist well to remove excess water from it.
3. Transfer zucchini to a cleaned bowl, add remaining ingredients and then stir until combined.
4. Switch on the air fryer, insert fryer basket, line it with perforated baking paper, grease it with non-stick cooking oil spray, then shut with its lid, set the fryer at 360 degrees F, and preheat for 5 minutes.
5. Open the fryer, spoon the zucchini mixture in the air fryer basket in a single layer, spray oil on the food, close with its lid and cook for 12 minutes until thoroughly cooked and golden brown, turning halfway.
6. Serve straight away.

Nutrition Value:

- Calories: 57 Cal
- Fat: 1 g
- Carbs: 8 g
- Protein: 3 g
- Fiber: 1 g

Zucchini and Summer Squash

Preparation time: 5 minutes
Cooking time: 8 minutes
Servings: 6

Ingredients:

- 2 large zucchini, sliced lengthwise
- ½ teaspoon salt
- 2 large summer squash, sliced lengthwise
- ¼ teaspoon crushed red pepper
- ¼ teaspoon ground black pepper
- 1 teaspoon lemon zest
- 2 tablespoons olive oil

Method:

1. Switch on the air fryer, insert fryer basket, grease it with non-stick cooking oil spray, then shut with its lid, set the fryer at 400 degrees F, and preheat for 5 minutes.
2. Meanwhile, take a shallow dish, place vegetable slices in it, add remaining ingredients and then toss until coated.
3. Open the fryer, arrange vegetable slices in the air fryer basket in a single layer, close with its lid and cook for 8 minutes until thoroughly cooked and crispy, turning halfway.
4. Serve straight away.

Nutrition Value:

- Calories: 147 Cal
- Fat: 11 g
- Carbs: 11 g
- Protein: 2 g
- Fiber: 3 g

Zucchini, Onion, and Yellow Squash

Preparation time: 5 minutes
Cooking time: 15 minutes
Servings: 4

Ingredients:

- 2 medium zucchini, ¼-inch sliced
- ¼ teaspoon salt
- 2 medium yellow squash, ¼-inch sliced
- ¼ teaspoon garlic powder
- 1 medium white onion, peeled, diced
- ¼ teaspoon ground black pepper
- 4 tablespoons olive oil

Method:

1. Switch on the air fryer, insert fryer basket, grease it with non-stick cooking oil spray, then shut with its lid, set the fryer at 400 degrees F, and preheat for 5 minutes.
2. Meanwhile, take a large bowl, place all the vegetable slices in it, add remaining ingredients and then toss until coated.
3. Open the fryer, arrange vegetable slices in the air fryer basket in a single layer, close with its lid and cook for 15 minutes until thoroughly cooked and crispy, turning halfway.
4. Serve straight away.

Nutrition Value:

- Calories: 88 Cal
- Fat: 5 g
- Carbs: 9 g
- Protein: 3 g
- Fiber: 2.5 g

Brussels Sprouts

Preparation time: 5 minutes
Cooking time: 14 minutes
Servings: 2

Ingredients:

- 2 cups Brussels sprouts
- ¼ teaspoon sea salt
- 1 tablespoon balsamic vinegar
- 1 tablespoon olive oil

Method:

1. Switch on the air fryer, insert fryer basket, grease it with non-stick cooking oil spray, then shut with its lid, set the fryer at 400 degrees F, and preheat for 5 minutes.
2. Meanwhile, take a large bowl, place all the ingredients in it and then toss until mixed.
3. Open the fryer, arrange the Brussels sprouts in the air fryer basket in a single layer, close with its lid and cook for 14 minutes until thoroughly cooked and golden brown, turning halfway.
4. Serve straight away.

Nutrition Value:

- Calories: 212.7 Cal
- Fat: 6.9 g
- Carbs: 24.2 g
- Protein: 5.8 g
- Fiber: 9.8 g

Cauliflower Fritters

Preparation time: 5 minutes
Cooking time: 15 minutes
Servings: 1

Ingredients:

- ½ cup cauliflower rice
- 1 tablespoon vegan grated parmesan cheese
- ¼ teaspoon ranch dressing mix
- ¼ cup vegan grated mozzarella cheese

Method:

1. Switch on the air fryer, insert fryer basket, line it with perforated baking paper, grease it with non-stick cooking oil spray, then shut with its lid, set the fryer at 425 degrees F, and preheat for 5 minutes.
2. Meanwhile, take a medium bowl, place all the ingredients in it and then stir until combined.
3. Open the fryer, mound the cauliflower mixture in the air fryer basket in a single layer, spread each mound like a pancake, spray oil on the food, close with its lid and cook for 15 minutes until crisp, turning halfway.
4. Serve straight away.

Nutrition Value:

- Calories: 62.9 Cal
- Fat: 3.6 g
- Carbs: 2.4 g
- Protein: 5.3 g
- Fiber: 1 g

Spiced Okra Fries

Preparation time: 5 minutes
Cooking time: 15 minutes
Servings: 4

Ingredients:

- 15 ounces okra, fresh
- ½ teaspoon garlic powder
- 1 teaspoon paprika
- 1 teaspoon red chili powder
- 2 tablespoons olive oil

Method:

1. Switch on the air fryer, insert fryer basket, grease it with non-stick cooking oil spray, then shut with its lid, set the fryer at 400 degrees F, and preheat for 5 minutes.
2. Meanwhile, take a large bowl, place okra in it, add remaining ingredients and then toss until coated.
3. Open the fryer, arrange okra in the air fryer basket in a single layer, close with its lid and cook for 15 minutes until thoroughly cooked, turning halfway.
4. Serve straight away.

Nutrition Value:

- Calories: 100 Cal
- Fat: 7 g
- Carbs: 9 g
- Protein: 2 g
- Fiber: 4 g

Grilled Tomatoes

Preparation time: 5 minutes
Cooking time: 50 minutes
Servings: 2

Ingredients:

- 1 pound cherry tomatoes, halved height-wise

Method:

1. Switch on the air fryer, insert fryer basket, grease it with non-stick cooking oil spray, then shut with its lid, set the fryer at 240 degrees F, and preheat for 5 minutes.
2. Open the fryer, arrange tomato halves in the air fryer basket in a single layer, spray oil on the food, close with its lid and cook for 45 minutes until thoroughly cooked and half of their original size.
3. Then switch the temperature of air fryer to 390 degrees F and continue frying the tomatoes for 5 minutes.
4. Serve straight away.

Nutrition Value:

- Calories: 28.9 Cal
- Fat: 1.4 g
- Carbs: 2 g
- Protein: 0.4 g
- Fiber: 0.4 g

Spaghetti Squash Fritters

Preparation time: 10 minutes
Cooking time: 8 minutes
Servings: 4

Ingredients:

- 2 cups air-fried spaghetti squash
- ¼ cup coconut flour
- ½ teaspoon garlic powder
- 2 teaspoons sliced green onion
- 1 teaspoon dried parsley
- 1 egg
- 1 teaspoon olive oil

Method:

1. Switch on the air fryer, insert fryer basket, grease it with non-stick cooking oil spray, then shut with its lid, set the fryer at 400 degrees F, and preheat for 5 minutes.
2. Meanwhile, wrap air-fried spaghetti squash in a cheesecloth and then twist it well to remove excess water.
3. Take a large bowl, place spaghetti squash in it, add remaining ingredients, stir until combined and then shape the mixture into 4 evenly sized patties.
4. Open the fryer, arrange squash patties in the air fryer basket in a single layer, close with its lid and cook for 8 minutes until thoroughly cooked and golden brown, turning halfway.
5. Serve straight away.

Nutrition Value:

- Calories: 131 Cal
- Fat: 10.1 g
- Carbs: 5.1 g
- Protein: 3.8 g
- Fiber: 2 g

Spaghetti Squash

Preparation time: 5 minutes
Cooking time: 30 minutes
Servings: 4

Ingredients:

- 1 large spaghetti squash, halved, deseeded
- 1 teaspoon salt
- ½ teaspoon ground black pepper
- 1 teaspoon olive oil

Method:

1. Switch on the air fryer, insert fryer basket, grease it with non-stick cooking oil spray, then shut with its lid, set the fryer at 360 degrees F, and preheat for 5 minutes.
2. Meanwhile, brush the squash halves with oil and then season with salt and black pepper.
3. Open the fryer, arrange squash halves cut-side-up in the air fryer basket in a single layer, close with its lid and cook for 30minutes until thoroughly cooked.
4. Serve straight away.

Nutrition Value:

- Calories: 42 Cal
- Fat: 0.4 g
- Carbs: 10 g
- Protein: 1 g
- Fiber: 2.2 g

Latkes

Preparation time: 10 minutes
Cooking time: 12 minutes
Servings: 20

Ingredients:

- 1 ½ pound rutabaga, shredded
- ½ of medium white onion, peeled, finely chopped
- 2 teaspoons salt
- ¼ cup oats
- ½ teaspoon ground black pepper
- 2 eggs

Method:

1. Switch on the air fryer, insert fryer basket, grease it with non-stick cooking oil spray, then shut with its lid, set the fryer at 375 degrees F, and preheat for 5 minutes.
2. Meanwhile, wrap shredded rutabaga and onion in a kitchen towel and then twist to remove liquid in it.
3. Take a large bowl, place rutabaga and onion in it, add remaining ingredients and then stir until combined.
4. Spoon the rutabaga mixture in the air fryer basket in a single layer, close with its lid and cook for 12 minutes until thoroughly cooked and golden brown, turning halfway.
5. Serve straight away.

Nutrition Value:

- Calories: 206 Cal
- Fat: 13 g
- Carbs: 19.2 g
- Protein: 3.5 g
- Fiber: 1.2 g

Cauliflower Wings

Preparation time: 10 minutes
Cooking time: 18 minutes
Servings: 4

Ingredients:

- 1 large head of cauliflower, cut into florets
- 1 teaspoon cornstarch
- 1 teaspoon onion powder
- 1 teaspoon garlic salt
- 1 cup coconut flour
- ½ teaspoon salt
- 1 teaspoon smoked paprika
- 1 teaspoon white vinegar
- ½ teaspoon ground black pepper
- 2 tablespoons vegan butter, melted
- ½ cup Buffalo Sauce
- 1 cup almond milk, unsweetened

Method:

1. Switch on the air fryer, insert fryer basket, grease it with non-stick cooking oil spray, then shut with its lid, set the fryer at 400 degrees F, and preheat for 5 minutes.
2. Meanwhile, take a medium saucepan, place it over medium heat, pour in milk, whisk in cornstarch until smooth and then cook the mixture for 5 minutes until slightly thickened.
3. Meanwhile, take a large bowl, place flour in it, add garlic salt, onion powder, salt, black pepper and paprika and then stir until mixed.
4. Working on one floret at a time, dredge in flour mixture, dip in milk mixture and then dredge in flour mixture until coated.
5. Open the fryer, arrange the cauliflower florets in the air fryer basket in a single layer, spray oil on the food, close with its lid and cook for 8 minutes until thoroughly cooked and golden brown, turning halfway.
6. Meanwhile, prepare the sauce and for this, take a small saucepan, place it over medium heat, add butter, vinegar and buffalo sauce, whisk until combined and then cook until butter melts and sauce begin to simmer.
7. When cauliflower florets have fried, toss them into the prepared sauce and then serve.

Nutrition Value:

- Calories: 357 Cal
- Fat: 18.8 g
- Carbs: 39.4 g
- Protein: 10.6 g
- Fiber: 6.5 g

Fried Radish

Preparation time: 5 minutes
Cooking time: 10 minutes
Servings: 4

Ingredients:

- 16 ounces radish
- 1 tablespoon seasoning salt
- 1 tablespoon ground black pepper
- 1 ½ tablespoon olive oil

Method:

1. Switch on the air fryer, insert fryer basket, grease it with non-stick cooking oil spray, then shut with its lid, set the fryer at 390 degrees F, and preheat for 5 minutes.
2. Meanwhile, take a medium bowl, place radish in it, drizzle with oil and then toss until coated.
3. Sprinkle with salt and black pepper, and then toss until coated.
4. Open the fryer, arrange radish in the air fryer basket in a single layer, close with its lid and cook for 7 to 10 minutes until thoroughly cooked, turning halfway.
5. Serve straight away.

Nutrition Value:

- Calories: 59 Cal
- Fat: 5 g
- Carbs: 4 g
- Protein: 1 g
- Fiber: 2 g

Radish Chips

Preparation time: 10 minutes
Cooking time: 8 minutes
Servings: 4

Ingredients:

- 2 bunches of radish, thinly sliced
- ½ teaspoon onion powder
- ¼ teaspoon salt
- ½ teaspoon garlic powder
- ¼ teaspoon ground black pepper
- 1 tablespoon dried parsley
- 2 tablespoons olive oil
- 2 cups water

Method:

1. Take a medium saucepan, pour in water, place it over medium-high heat and then bring it to a boil.
2. Add slices of radish, boil for 5 minutes until translucent, drain the radish slices and then pat dry with paper towels.
3. Switch on the air fryer, insert fryer basket, grease it with non-stick cooking oil spray, then shut with its lid, set the fryer at 320 degrees F, and preheat for 5 minutes.
4. Meanwhile, take a medium bowl, place radish slices in it, add remaining ingredients and then toss until coated.
5. Open the fryer, arrange radish slices in the air fryer basket in a single layer, spray oil on the food, close with its lid and cook for 8 minutes until thoroughly cooked, turning halfway.
6. Serve straight away.

Nutrition Value:

- Calories: 77 Cal
- Fat: 6.5 g
- Carbs: 2.2 g
- Protein: 0.8 g
- Fiber: 1.8 g

Yellow Squash

Preparation time: 5 minutes
Cooking time: 10 minutes
Servings: 4

Ingredients:

- 2 medium yellow squash, peeled, cored, ¾-inch sliced
- ¼ teaspoon salt
- 1/8 teaspoon ground black pepper
- 2 teaspoons olive oil

Method:

1. Switch on the air fryer, insert fryer basket, grease it with non-stick cooking oil spray, then shut with its lid, set the fryer at 400 degrees F, and preheat for 5 minutes.
2. Meanwhile, take a large bowl, place squash slices in it, add remaining ingredients and then toss until coated.
3. Open the fryer, arrange squash slices in the air fryer basket in a single layer, close with its lid and cook for 8 to 10 minutes until thoroughly cooked and golden brown, turning halfway.
4. Serve straight away.

Nutrition Value:

- Calories: 21 Cal
- Fat: 2.4 g
- Carbs: 0.2 g
- Protein: 0.2 g
- Fiber: 0.05 g

Fried Green Tomatoes

Preparation time: 5 minutes
Cooking time: 15 minutes
Servings: 6

Ingredients:

- 2 green tomatoes, ¼-inch thick slices
- 1/3 cup coconut flour
- 1 cup oats
- 1 teaspoon garlic powder
- ¼ teaspoon salt and more as needed
- ½ teaspoon paprika
- ¼ teaspoon ground black pepper
- 1 tablespoon olive oil
- ½ cup buttermilk
- 2 eggs

Method:

1. Switch on the air fryer, insert fryer basket, grease it with non-stick cooking oil spray, then shut with its lid, set the fryer at 400 degrees F, and preheat for 5 minutes.
2. Meanwhile, take a shallow dish and place flour in it.
3. Take a separate shallow dish, crack eggs in it, pour in the buttermilk and then whisk until blended.
4. Take a separate shallow dish, place oats in it, add garlic powder, salt and paprika and then stir until mixed.
5. Season the slices of tomatoes with salt and black pepper and then, working on one slice at a time, coat in flour, dip into the eggs and then dredge in oats mixture until coated.
6. Open the fryer, arrange tomato slices in the air fryer basket in a single layer, close with its lid and cook for 15 minutes until thoroughly cooked and golden brown, turning halfway.
7. Serve straight away.

Nutrition Value:

- Calories: 219.2 Cal
- Fat: 5.3 g
- Carbs: 39.6 g
- Protein: 7.6 g
- Fiber: 1.7 g

Jicama Fries

Preparation time: 5 minutes
Cooking time: 15 minutes
Servings: 1

Ingredients:

- 1 medium jicama, peeled, cut into matchsticks
- ½ teaspoon garlic powder
- ¾ teaspoon salt
- 1 teaspoon paprika
- ½ teaspoon ground black pepper
- 2 tablespoons olive oil

Method:

1. Switch on the air fryer, insert fryer basket, grease it with non-stick cooking oil spray, then shut with its lid, set the fryer at 400 degrees F, and preheat for 5 minutes.
2. Meanwhile, take a large bowl, place jicama pieces in it, add remaining ingredients and then toss until combined.
3. Open the fryer, arrange jicama pieces in the air fryer basket in a single layer, close with its lid and cook for 15 minutes until thoroughly cooked, tossing every 5 minutes.
4. Serve straight away.

Nutrition Value:

- Calories: 125 Cal
- Fat: 7 g
- Carbs: 15 g
- Protein: 1 g
- Fiber: 8 g

Fried Zucchini and Yellow Squash

Preparation time: 20 minutes
Cooking time: 8 minutes
Servings: 8

Ingredients:

- 1 medium zucchini, sliced
- 2 cups coconut flour
- 1 medium yellow squash, sliced
- 1 teaspoon salt
- 2 cups oats
- 2 eggs
- 1 cup buttermilk

Method:

1. Take a large bowl, place zucchini and squash slices in it, pour in the milk and then let the vegetables soak for 15 minutes.
2. Take a shallow dish and place coconut flour in it.
3. Take a separate shallow dish, crack the eggs in it and then whisk until beaten.
4. Take a separate dish and then place oats in it.
5. When ready to cook, switch on the air fryer, insert fryer basket, grease it with non-stick cooking oil spray, then shut with its lid, set the fryer at 390 degrees F, and preheat for 5 minutes.
6. Meanwhile, working on one vegetable slice at a time, dredge in flour, dip into the egg and then dredge in oats until coated.
7. Open the fryer, arrange vegetable slices in the air fryer basket in a single layer, close with its lid and cook for 8 minutes until thoroughly cooked and crispy, turning halfway.
8. Serve straight away.

Nutrition Value:

- Calories: 334 Cal
- Fat: 4 g
- Carbs: 62 g
- Protein: 12 g
- Fiber: 4 g

Eggplant

Preparation time: 10 minutes
Cooking time: 20 minutes
Servings: 4

Ingredients:

- 1 ½ pound eggplant, ½-inch cubed
- 1 teaspoon garlic powder
- 1 tablespoon salt
- ½ teaspoon dried oregano
- ¼ teaspoon ground black pepper
- ¼ teaspoon dried thyme
- 1 teaspoon paprika
- 2 tablespoons vegetable broth

Method:

1. Place eggplant pieces in a colander, sprinkle with salt, toss until mixed and then let them rest for 30 minutes.
2. Then drain the eggplant pieces, pat dry with paper towels and place in a large bowl.
3. Add remaining ingredients into a large bowl and then toss until mixed.
4. Switch on the air fryer, insert fryer basket, grease it with non-stick cooking oil spray, then shut with its lid, set the fryer at 380 degrees F, and preheat for 5 minutes.
5. Open the fryer, arrange the eggplant pieces in the air fryer basket, spray oil on the food, close with its lid and cook for 20 minutes until thoroughly cooked and golden brown, turning halfway.
6. Serve straight away.

Nutrition Value:

- Calories: 48 Cal
- Fat: 1 g
- Carbs: 11 g
- Protein: 2 g
- Fiber: 5 g

Stuffed Tomatoes

Preparation time: 5 minutes
Cooking time: 25 minutes
Servings: 4

Ingredients:

- 4 large tomatoes
- ¼ cup minced onion
- ½ pound ground chicken, extra-lean
- ¾ cup oats
- 1 teaspoon minced garlic
- 1 teaspoon salt and more as needed
- ¼ cup chopped basil
- ½ teaspoon ground black pepper
- 1 cup vegan shredded mozzarella cheese
- 1 tablespoon olive oil
- ¼ cup vegan grated parmesan cheese

Method:

1. Cut off the top of each tomato, remove its seeds and insides and then season with salt.
2. Take a plate, line it with paper towels, place tomatoes upside-down on it and let them rest until drained completely.
3. Meanwhile, prepare the filling and for this, take a large skillet pan, place it over medium-high heat, add oil and when hot, add onion and garlic and then cook for 2 minutes.
4. Add ground chicken and continue cooking it for 8 minutes until nicely browned and cooked.
5. Then remove the pan from heat, add oats, basil and both cheeses and stir until combined.
6. Switch on the air fryer, insert fryer basket, grease it with non-stick cooking oil spray, then shut with its lid, set the fryer at 350 degrees F, and preheat for 5 minutes.
7. Meanwhile, season tomatoes with black pepper and some more salt and then fill their cavity with the cooked chicken mixture until stuffed.
8. Open the fryer, arrange stuffed tomatoes in the air fryer basket in a single layer, spray oil on the food, close with its lid and cook for 10 minutes until thoroughly cooked and cheese have melted, turning halfway.
9. Serve straight away.

Nutrition Value:

- Calories: 180 Cal
- Fat: 7 g
- Carbs: 14 g
- Protein: 16 g
- Fiber: 4 g

Roasted Turnips

Preparation time: 5 minutes
Cooking time: 25 minutes
Servings: 4

Ingredients:

- 4 medium turnips, peeled, diced
- 1 teaspoon sea salt
- 1 ½ teaspoon paprika
- 1 teaspoon ground black pepper
- 2 teaspoons olive oil
- 2 teaspoons minced parsley

Method:

1. Switch on the air fryer, insert fryer basket, grease it with non-stick cooking oil spray, then shut with its lid, set the fryer at 390 degrees F, and preheat for 5 minutes.
2. Meanwhile, take a medium bowl, place turnips pieces in it, add remaining ingredients except for the parsley and then stir until combined.
3. Open the fryer, arrange turnip pieces in the air fryer basket in a single layer, close with its lid and cook for 25 minutes until thoroughly cooked and golden brown, turning halfway.
4. Serve straight away.

Nutrition Value:

- Calories: 51 Cal
- Fat: 3 g
- Carbs: 9 g
- Protein: 1 g
- Fiber: 3 g

Turnip Fries

Preparation time: 5 minutes
Cooking time: 20 minutes
Servings: 4

Ingredients:

- 2 pounds turnips, peeled, cut to ½-inch sticks
- 2 tablespoons cornstarch
- ½ teaspoon onion powder
- 1 teaspoon garlic powder
- ½ teaspoon salt
- ¼ teaspoon ground black pepper
- 1 teaspoon paprika
- 2 tablespoons olive oil

Method:

1. Switch on the air fryer, insert fryer basket, grease it with non-stick cooking oil spray, then shut with its lid, set the fryer at 400 degrees F, and preheat for 5 minutes.
2. Meanwhile, take a large bowl, place turnips in it, sprinkle with cornstarch and then toss until coated.
3. Take a small bowl, add salt, black pepper, onion powder, garlic powder, paprika and oil and then stir until combined.
4. Drizzle this mixture over the turnips and then toss until coated.
5. Open the fryer, arrange turnip sticks in the air fryer basket in a single layer, close with its lid and cook for 20 minutes until thoroughly cooked and crispy, turning halfway.
6. Serve straight away.

Nutrition Value:

- Calories: 115 Cal
- Fat: 4.3 g
- Carbs: 18.2 g
- Protein: 0.8 g
- Fiber: 4.8 g

Chapter 8: 30-Day Meal Plan

Day 1

Breakfast: Kale Deviled Eggs

Lunch: Venison Bites

Dinner: Buttermilk Fried Mushrooms

Day 2

Breakfast: Oatmeal Muffins

Lunch: Chicken and Vegetables Fried Rice

Dinner: Pulled Pork

Day 3

Breakfast: Muffinless Egg Cups

Lunch: Cauliflower Fritters

Dinner: Salmon and Asparagus

Day 4

Breakfast: Tempeh

Lunch: Yellow Squash

Dinner: Chicken Nuggets

Day 5

Breakfast: Sausage and Egg Breakfast Cups

Lunch: Crispy Pork Chops

Dinner: Garlic and Lemon Fish

Day 6

Breakfast: Sausages

Lunch: Naked Chicken Tenders

Dinner: Spiced Okra Fries

Day 7

Breakfast: Broccoli Frittata

Lunch: Turkey Breast

Dinner: Fish Cakes with Cilantro

Day 8

Breakfast: Quiche

Lunch: Cauliflower Wings

Dinner: Cracklin' Chicken

Day 9

Breakfast: Tofu Spinach Sauté

Lunch: Garlic Chicken Tenders

Dinner: Zucchini Fritters

Day 10

Breakfast: Egg White Muffin Cups with Peppers

Lunch: Latkes

Dinner: Pork Loin

Day 11

Breakfast: Chocolate Chip and Oatmeal Cookies

Lunch: Cornish Hens

Dinner: Artichoke Hearts

Day 12

Breakfast: Lentil Sliders

Lunch: Salmon Cakes

Dinner: Breaded Chicken Breasts

Day 13

Breakfast: Sausage Patties

Lunch: Turkey Burgers

Dinner: Spaghetti Squash Fritters

Day 14

Breakfast: Tofu Scramble

Lunch: Chicken Cauliflower Fried Rice

Dinner: Pecan Crusted Halibut

Day 15

Breakfast: Egg White Muffins

Lunch: Roast Duck

Dinner: Zucchini Strips

Day 16

Breakfast: Spinach Frittata

Lunch: Seasoned Rutabaga Fries

Dinner: Buttermilk Chicken

Day 17

Breakfast: Crustless Mini Taco Quiche

Lunch: Hasselback Fajita Chicken

Dinner: Fried Radish

Day 18

Breakfast: Kale Deviled Eggs

Lunch: Spiced Pork Chops with Broccoli

Dinner: Venison Burgers

Day 19

Breakfast: Oatmeal Muffins

Lunch: Fish Skewers

Dinner: Cabbage Fritters

Day 20

Breakfast: Muffinless Egg Cups

Lunch: Brussels Sprouts

Dinner: Crab Cakes

Day 21

Breakfast: Tempeh

Lunch: Ranch Chicken Tenders

Dinner: Pork Tenderloin

Day 22

Breakfast: Sausage and Egg Breakfast Cups

Lunch: Lemon and Garlic Salmon

Dinner: Tender Chicken Breasts

Day 23

Breakfast: Sausages

Lunch: Pork Chops with Brussels Sprouts

Dinner: Crustless Chicken and Spinach Quiche

Day 24

Breakfast: Broccoli Frittata

Lunch: Breaded Pork Chops

Dinner: Lemon Pepper Shrimp

Day 25

Breakfast: Quiche

Lunch: Eggplant

Dinner: Glazed Pork Tenderloin

Day 26

Breakfast: Tofu Spinach Sauté

Lunch: Stuffed Tomatoes

Dinner: Crispy Chicken Dinner

Day 27

Breakfast: Egg White Muffin Cups with Peppers

Lunch: Super Quick Pork Chops

Dinner: Zucchini and Summer Squash

Day 28

Breakfast: Chocolate Chip and Oatmeal Cookies

Lunch: Blackened Tilapia Fillets

Dinner: Garlic Butter Pork Chops

Day 29

Breakfast: Lentil Sliders

Lunch: Cajun Salmon

Dinner: Crispy Ranch Fish

Day 30

Breakfast: Sausage Patties

Lunch: Fish Sticks

Dinner: Southern Style Pork Chops

Conclusion

This excellent cookbook not only contains 800-Day Super Easy Air Fryer Recipes that you can make right in Optavia Air Fryer in just a matter of minutes, but also the secrets to unlocking the fryer's true potential that few people use! No more improvising with Optavia Air Fryer, no more using obsolete recipes.

Now you can save time, money, and start eating healthier versions of your favorite foods using your fryer's full power, thanks to this revolutionary cookbook!

Stop wasting your time trying to find delicious and healthy recipes. Grab a copy of this cookbook and start enjoying the crunch without the calories and messy cleanup with Optavia Air Fryer Cookbook for beginners!